WHAT IF...?

Indian Cricket's Counter-Factual History

BY
GULU EZEKIEL

Edited by
Sachin Bajaj

ISBN
Paperback 979-8-89724-993-0
Hardcase 979-8-89906-593-4

Front cover:
Tiger Pataudi, Dilip Sardesai, Nari Contractor, Salim Durani.

Back cover:
Author with Kapil Dev.

All photos author's personal collection.
Inside cover photo of author by Vinod Sharma.

Dedication

Dedicated to my beloved parents Prof. Joe Ezekiel and Khorshed Wadia Ezekiel. May their memories be a blessing.

PUBLISHER'S NOTE

By Sachin Bajaj

With this unique and fascinating book, I am delighted to welcome Gulu Ezekiel to the Global Cricket School family. I have known Gulu for over 20 years during which he has written numerous books which have received acclaim throughout the cricket world. These include biographies of Sachin Tendulkar, Sourav Ganguly, Mahendra Singh Dhoni and late Salim Durani. I am sure this will be the first of many more by Gulu for GCS.

Contents

Introduction

By Gulu Ezekiel

The pathway to this book began in the 1970s through *Marvel Comics,* a joint passion with cricket in my teen years. My favourite superheroes were part of a series of comics titled just that, 'What If?', now an online animated series. The comics ran from 1977 to 1984 and featured alternative scenarios if certain events had occurred differently.

This format has also been applied to movies, TV shows and even historical books over the years. But all those years after the comics first appeared I would be sub-consciously looking at alternative scenarios to cricket events over the past six decades.

When I read famed cricket and Gandhi historian Ramachandra Guha's column on this theme in *The Telegraph,* Kolkata ('Cricketing Might-Have-Beens', May 28, 2005) it fired up my enthusiasm for the subject all over again. I mailed Ramachandra and we discussed the topic.

In 2022 when I was first seriously mulling writing this book—other projects subsequently took precedence—I contacted Ramachandra as I could not find the column online and he very kindly retrieved it for me from his computer.

A few years later *The Cricketer* monthly of UK began a series of features on the topic by cricket writers around the world with my contribution being on Mansur Ali Khan Pataudi (September 2017).

Understandably being a UK publication most of the themes centred round English cricket and The Ashes. It ran from April 2017 to 2019 though the first article on the subject actually appeared in the May 2016 issue (on the subject of DRS—Decision Review System).

Gideon Haigh also contributed an article on the theme for *The Cricket Monthly* ('Kapil Drops Richards', January 2015).

Most of the contributions to *The Cricketer* and Haigh's article too vividly painted the alternative scenario as if it had actually happened.

Outlook magazine brought out a What If…Collector's Issue (August 22, 2004) which dealt with mainly political topics and one sport 'What If We Had Lost?', that being the 1983 Prudential World Cup final against West Indies.

I decided to veer away from that style—fiction in any case is neither my cup of tea nor my forte.

Instead I have traced historical incidents from Indian cricket, briefly placed before the reader what may have happened if events had turned out differently—but then left the rest to their imagination.

Along the way I have narrated the history of Indian cricket from the earliest days to the present from a unique angle. It has been a fascinating journey for me and I trust the readers will find it an even more fascinating experience going through the book which is the first of its kind.

Of course cricket fans can narrate hundreds, even thousands of such scenarios. My task has been picking what I consider the most impactful on Indian and world cricket. I am sure readers will have their own favourites too.

The theme is an esoteric one as is the genre known as counter-factual history and not many I discussed it with could understand the theme.

My thanks therefore to my publisher Sachin Bajaj who immediately grasped its essence and expressed full faith in my ability to flesh it out in a book—the first of its kind.

Postscript: Even as this book was being completed, came the news that stand-in captain and pace ace Jasprit Bumrah's absence with injury for the fifth and final Test at Sydney in the Border-Gavaskar Trophy after bowling just 10 overs meant Australia romped to victory and sealed the series 3-1. In those 60 balls Bumrah grabbed two wickets before going off with back spasms? **What if** he had been fit to bowl right through? Australia's target of 162 would have been a very steep hill to climb since this was (in Bumrah's poignant words post-Test) "the spiciest wicket in the series". The series would then have been deadlocked 2-2 and India would have retained the Trophy which was already in their possession. Bumrah finished with 32 wickets in the series, the most for an Indian abroad and just three behind BS Chandrasekhar's record of 35 in 1972-73. An agonizing **What if** for Indian cricket for sure!

—New Delhi, January 2025

Note:

1. Since this is a historical narrative, I have used the original names of cities—i.e. Bangalore, Bombay, Calcutta, Madras, Poona, etc.

2. All events and records unless specifically stated pertain to men's cricket only.

3. Though the name of the community is spelt both as Parsee and Parsi, I have used the former as prevalent in early cricket literature on India.

4. All statistics updated till end of the 2024-25 Border-Gavaskar Trophy

CHAPTER ONE

Parsees the Pioneers

How cricket started in India—and almost ended.
Plus, an Ashes close shave.

The year was 1721. Britannia was already ruling the waves and for the next two centuries would waive the rules in its colonial conquests. India of course was the jewel—and not just the pilfered Kohinoor—in the British crown.

Wherever the British planted their flag cricket was not far away and it was their sailors who flew the flag of both Britain and cricket.

Even though its origins can be traced back to the 16th century, it was not till 1624 that the first match in England came to be recorded. Till then restricted to the British Isles, the first instance of it being played abroad was in 1676 in the unlikely city of Aleppo in Syria, specifically at Green Plat, about 6 miles from the city. And the date of the game as recorded in his diary by British sailor Henry Teonge was May 6, 1676.

India in 1721 was thus the second country outside Britain to witness a game of cricket, inevitably by its sailors though in the somewhat unlikely village of Tankari Bandar (Bandar means port in Gujarati), on the banks of the river Dhadhar about 50 miles from Vadodara.

Even as the East India Company spread their tentacles and set down their roots with HQ in Calcutta, it was in the capital of Bengal (and of imperial India till it shifted to Delhi in 1911) that the British set up the Calcutta Cricket Club (CCC).

Dates vary between 1792 and 1825. But former Bengal and East Zone captain Raju Mukherji in his book *Eden Gardens: Legends and Romance* reproduced a page from India's first English newspaper, *Hickey's Bengal Gazette* (established 1780) that reports (in its 48th edition dated Saturday, December 16 to Saturday, December 23, 1780) a function held at the CCC. Though the event described was a feast, the report specifically names the CCC. The year 1780 is significant as the game's most prominent club, the Marylebone Cricket Club (MCC) was established in 1787. And while the first recorded match played by the CCC has been traced to 1792, it is only logical to believe a club with cricket in its name was formed for the express purpose of playing the game.

Of course cricket was the exclusive preserve of the ruling British elite and no Indians (nor dogs)—save for the menial staff—were allowed to set foot in their posh clubs.

The Parsees Step In

The minuscule Parsee community is perhaps the best loved of all in India, punching far above their numbers when it comes to their contribution to the growth of India in practically every field including cricket (11 male Test cricketers including two captains and many women too including the legendary Diana Eduljee. Remarkable since their number in India barely crossed 100,000 at its peak in 1940).

In the words of scholar, historian and cricketer (Ranji Trophy for Bihar) Dr. Sujit Mukherjee in his wonderful book *Between Indian Wickets* (page 48): "In cricket—as in industry or commerce or education, or philanthropy—the Parsi community's contribution to India's development and in these and other public causes has been utterly out of proportion to the size of the community."

Serendipitously, the community of Zoroastrian fire-worshippers from Persia (later Iran) who fled their native land to escape religious persecution from Arab invaders, first landed in Udvada off the Gujarat coast in the seventh century. This was another early link between Gujarat and cricket in India.

But **what if** they had not taken to cricket so enthusiastically that they were the first to send teams abroad, to England in 1886 and again in 1888? Would cricket in India never have taken off in the first place? And **what if** the Brits had succeeded in their nefarious plot to destroy Parsee cricket virtually at birth? Would cricket in India have died an early death? Read on…

It is true the Parsees initially took to this most British of sports to curry favour with the colonial rulers. But it was not long before they ran up against hostility and responded with how they knew best, by beating the Brits at their own game.

According to Vasant Raiji in *India's Hambledon Men,* Parsee schoolboys were receiving cricket coaching as early as 1839. These same players formed the first Indian cricket club in 1848. The Oriental CC then morphed two years later into the Young Zoroastrian Club which 175 years later is remarkably still in existence. The Hindu and Muslim communities followed with their own clubs in the 1860s but were not as active as the Parsees who took their new-found passion for cricket to the next level.

The big breakthrough came in 1876 when Ardeshir Byramji Patel founded the Parsee Cricket Club and pulled off a coup in arranging a match in the winter of 1877 with the Bombay Gymkhana which was then exclusively White European. This in the same year as what is recognized as the first-ever Test match at Melbourne between England and Australia.

The natives lost the single innings match by 63 runs, 168 to 105. The scorecard for this match is not available.

But there was another one in 1877 (October 15, 16) which is available at *cricketarchive.com* (run by the Association of Cricket Statisticians). It shows "match drawn (Parsees won on first innings)." It also mentions "match was scheduled for one day but extended to two."

Brief scores (at Bombay Gymkhana, Oct. 15, 16, 1877): Parsees 140 (RJ Kapadia 39) and 76 (B. Bhicajee 17) v. Bombay Gymkhana 93 (W. Maule 26 not out, DH Patel 7-41) and 41 for two. So that was a remarkable achievement.

Emboldened, Patel now turned his attention to England, then the Mecca of cricket. This was hugely ambitious as no cricket team had crossed the seas to play outside India.

Dr. Sujit Mukherjee again from the same book (page 51): "It is difficult for us today to imagine the kind of initiative, confidence and enterprise owned by these men, as yet in their infancy of cricket, who even conceived of such an undertaking."

When news reached England of these plans the *London Graphic* (10 August 1878) reported: "It is not everywhere, however, that John Bull finds any of the natives to join in the sport; they are generally content to 'assist' by simply looking on. There are nevertheless, exceptions to the rule, and in the Bombay Presidency the Parsees, who have long shown themselves superior to the prejudices with which other Indian races are more or less fettered, have come out quite strong as cricketers. Before long it is rumoured a Parsee eleven will visit our shores for the purpose of contending with us on our native turf. We have already received several severe drubbings in the cricket field from our Australian cousins, perhaps next we are to be knocked (cricketically) into a cocked hat by the descendants of the Fire Worshippers of Persia."

Not for the last time, the Parsee community's forward thinking was thwarted by a fellow-Parsee, KN Kabraji, leading to a libel suit, after which the tour was put on hold.

To add to their difficulties, instead of welcoming them into the fold, the British rulers poured scorn on the Parsee attempts at cricket and did everything in their powers to thwart their progress including mocking their habit of wearing their traditional clothing while playing. And thereby hangs a tale. For while the good showing of the Parsees against the Gymkhana team had fired the imagination of the community, it had the opposite effect on their opponents—in fact it got under the skin of the Raj and now came the bid to sabotage the Parsees' passion for cricket.

The first bid was in 1868 and was triggered by the stray incident of a ball hit by a Parsee batsman which brushed against the wife of a British police constable who was taking a stroll across the Oval maidan. This was enough for the Commissioner of Police, FS Soulter to forbid the Parsees from playing at the Oval. Despite sympathetic support from some eminent Englishmen, Soulter was unmoved and the Parsees lost that precious piece of playing field.

Then in 1879 more hurdles were placed in their way, no doubt a deliberate ploy to disrupt uppity Parsees who were now determined to take on the British at their own game.

It was the game of polo, ironically Persian in its origins, which became their vehicle of obstruction. The English polo players took up wide swathes of the Esplanade Parade ground on the open Maidan where Parsee teams played dozens of games of cricket simultaneously across the massive public field. It was Shapoorje Sorabjee who fired the first salvo by writing a letter of protest to the Bombay Gymkhana to which the polo teams belonged, on behalf of the Persian Cricket Club. The Polo Secretary promptly dismissed the complaint. The bitter tussle continued till the mid 1880s with petitions and counter petitions to the

Governor and letters to the leading newspapers flying back and forth, finally ending in defeat for the natives. They would now be confined to a tiny portion of the Maidan, that too roughed up by the polo ponies, making batting a dangerous act.

It left a bitter taste in the mouth of the community and made them more determined than ever.

The original idea behind taking to cricket—to curry favour with the British—was now turned on its head. From here on the Parsees vowed to teach them a lesson on the field of play.

Off to Blighty

The first step towards this came in 1886 when the community finally achieved their lofty ambition of taking a cricket team to England, the home and birthplace of cricket.

It was hardly a representative side though. Captained by Dr. Dunjeeshaw Heerjeebhoy Patel, it consisted of those players who could pay their own way.

The results were disastrous—played 28 matches, lost 19, won one, drew eight. But the idea was to learn from the masters and surely lessons were learned. Further, they were granted a match at Lord's where they came up against the giant of cricket, Dr. WG Grace who at 38 years was in his prime. The results were predictable—defeat by an innings with Grace doing the star turn with 11 wickets for 44 runs and MCC's second top-score of 65. MCC scored 313, the Parsees knocked over for 23 and 66.

Following the 1857 mutiny, India now came under the British crown and was no longer controlled by the East India Company. The royal-loving Parsees were thrilled to be invited by Queen Victoria to play a match at Cumberland Lodge in Windsor Great Park against The Prince's XI featuring two of her grandsons.

Wisden Cricketers' Almanack (founded in 1864) was dismissive of the tourists in its 1887 edition: "The tour of the Parsees: From a cricket point of view the tour of the Parsees was a failure, and we have not thought it worthwhile to print any of the scores. In arranging the fixtures, the powers of the players had been much overrated, and in the whole series of matches, the Parsees only gained one victory. Despite their ill-success, however, they thoroughly enjoyed the trip, and returned home with the pleasantest remembrances of English cricket and hospitality. We append the averages in batting and bowling of the most successful cricketers of the team."

But with just one season in between, the Parsees were back in England in 1888, obviously undaunted by the disastrous results of 1886.

There were only two of the 1888 team who had toured two years previously, Jal Merwanjee Morenas and Sorabjee Hormusjee Harwar. There was also a marked improvement in the results this time: Played 31, won eight, lost 11, drawn 12. *Wisden* though was once again dismissive, this time claiming the scores could not be published due to "want of space". But there was a word of praise for fast bowler Mehallasha Eduljee Pavri and his "wonderfully successful bowling"—170 wickets at the average of 11.11.

And Pavri it was who four years later shot the Parsee cricket team into the international headlines.

(Incidentally, the first cricket team from Australia to tour England in 1868 was made up entirely of Indigenous Australians)

Historic Win

What happened next galvanized cricket in India, inspired the Parsee community, caused euphoria around the country and shook the British Raj to the core. It also created one of the earliest—and most intriguing— **what if** scenarios in international cricket.

The first cricket team to tour India from abroad (1889-90) was GF Vernon's XI of county cricketers though the captain himself had played one Test in Australia. The team was originally to be led by the legendary Lord Hawke, but he fell ill and missed most of the matches and Vernon took over.

They travelled across Ceylon (now Sri Lanka) and India playing solely against India-based English cricketers, save for one match against the Parsees at Bombay Gymkhana on 30th and 31st January 1890. This was done more as a courtesy to the loyal Parsees whose past record in England both in 1886 and 1888 showed them as pushovers for the visitors with the betting odds heavily favouring the English team.

The Times of India correspondent though sounded a note of caution to the visitors: "The chances of cricket are such that if Mr. Vernon's XI take it too easy, or run away with the idea that they may hold their adversaries cheap, it is just possible that the Zoroastrians may score a victory after all."

Those words proved prophetic. The Gymkhana was packed with 12,000 spectators of all communities lustily cheering on the home side.

Batting first after winning the toss, the Englishmen were bowled out for 97 with the skipper (45 not out) scoring nearly half the total off his own bat. Such sub-100 totals were not unusual at a time when pitches were of poor quality and largely assisted the bowlers. Indeed at close of the first day's play the Parsees had tumbled to 80 for 9.

The *Times of India* reporter was more circumspect after the first day. "The visitors appeared to have recognized they had met with a rough lot, and though it is not generally felt that the Parsee team will win, yet the day's results portend a tough contest for the morrow."

The final Parsee wicket fell for the addition of just two runs on the second morning (a Friday), giving the visitors a lead of 15 runs.

While RE Modi and Dinshawji Patel opened the bowling in the first innings, captain JM Framjee Patel this time around brought in his star bowler Pavri (who got two wickets in the first innings) to open with Modi. Pavri had done the 'double' of 1,000 runs and 100 wickets on the 1888 tour.

The ploy worked wonders: in his very first over he had Edward Lawson-Smith (1) caught and bowled—one-handed at that—and in his next over bowled Arthur Gibson (6).

Vernon's (5) run out at 15 for three turned the match on its head and when Pavri bowled opener James Walker (2) at the same total, the tourists were in dire straits. Half the side were gone for a measly 20 runs when Modi got his first wicket and the crowd were now going wild with excitement—surely the Englishmen had no escape route left.

John Philipson decided to take the fight to the Parsee bowlers and cracked Pavri for three boundaries in one over. But he tried it once more and was caught at mid-on by captain Patel and Pavri now had four of the top six wickets in the bag. There was brief resistance by Albert Leatham whose 15 was the top score as the innings subsided for 61—leaving the delighted Parsees needing 77 for a famous landmark victory. It was the visitors' lowest total of the tour.

Pavri, according to Vasant Raiji, was the first star of Indian cricket, his massive physique coupled with an impressive beard giving him a formidable look. His outstanding figures of 7 for 34 had given his side more than a fighting chance

Pavri had opened the batting too in the first innings but in the second captain Patel promoted himself at the top with Morenas as his partner. But at 17 for four the Englishmen had fought their way back into the game.

It was Pavri again who thwarted them, this time with the bat. His 21 was the highest in the match for his team and the Parsees were home by four wickets.

The result bore an uncanny resemblance to India's first Test victory on English soil in the third Test at the Oval in 1971. Here too India won by four wickets with leg spinner BS Chandrasekhar's 6 for 38 in the second innings being the match-winner and here too a run out (England's Bombay-born opener John Jameson) proved vital in the second innings—remarkable coincidences 81 years apart. While at the Bombay Gymkhana it was DF Dubash who hit the winning runs—a boundary—at the Oval it was Syed Abid Ali who sealed the issue with a boundary too.

The immediate aftermath of the amazing victory was sheer pandemonium and euphoria at the ground The victors were the toast of Bombay, wined and dined by the rich and famous.

The Times of India in an editorial said the Parsees had "done honour to Bombay and all were proud of those who had held their own in tact and temper…"

WG Grace who was understandably skeptical after their disastrous tour of England in 1886 was suitably impressed this time around. "Six times they [Vernon's team] won in India in a single innings, and the clubs they played against were the strongest in India, which makes their defeat by the Parsee XI all the more remarkable."

The defeated captain and his team were stoic and sporting in defeat though other English observers were not so charitable, predicting dire consequences for the rulers being humbled by the natives at their own game.

It brought back bitter memories of the sarcastic comment made by the outgoing Governor of Bombay, Sir Philip Woodhouse in 1877 after the Parsees had been defeated by 63 runs in their first-ever match against the Bombay Gymkhana.

"While as for cricket, I have no doubt the Parsees expect to be able in a year or two to encounter an All England Eleven (laughter and applause)". This was resentfully recounted by Framjee Patel in his 1905 book *Stray Thoughts on Indian Cricket* (page 16).

Brief scores (Gymkhana ground, Bombay; 30, 31 January 1890): GF Vernon's XI 97 (GF Vernon 45 not out, BD Gagrat 4—29) and 62 (AE Leatham 15, ME Pavri 7—34), lost to Parsees 82 (JM Morenas 17, ER de Little 4-25) and 77 for six (Pavri 21), by four wickets.

Even *Wisden* was impressed enough in their 1891 edition to praise the Parsees for inflicting the sole defeat on the tourists on their long tour of Ceylon and India (Played 13, won 10, drawn two, lost one). "The game aroused the greatest interest, and success of the home eleven by four wickets was highly creditable."

The defeat of a strong visiting side by a team made up entirely of Indians was the first such sporting landmark on Indian soil.

It preceded by 21 years the victory of the Mohun Bagan Athletic Club against the East Yorkshire Regiment in the final of the Indian Football Association Shield in Calcutta in 1911 which has erroneously been given this exalted status, highly creditable though Mohun Bagan's win against all odds was.

That the victory by the Parsees was not a one-off was proved just three seasons later when Lord Hawke was back as captain and this time for the full tour.

Once again the tourists were beaten by the Parsees, this time by the handsome margin of 109 runs in Bombay in December 1892 and once again Pavri was the hero with eight wickets in the match including 6 for 36 in the second innings.

And to top it all, they again inflicted a rare defeat on the third English team to visit India in 1902-03, the Oxford University Authentics, with the indomitable Pavri once more playing his part.

Parsees Down Under? Not Quite

At this stage the reader may well wonder why I have gone into such details of these matches and what the significance is to the theme of the book. And herein hangs a tale of far-reaching consequences—in brief, **what if** the Parsees had toured Australia in 1893-94?

In 2027 the cricket world will celebrate the 150th anniversary of the birth of Test cricket, the first Test at Melbourne having been held between Australia and England in March 1877, though no one at the time was aware of the significance of the match listed as between J. Lillywhite's XI and the Australian Colonies. This was in fact the fourth visit by an English cricket team to Australia since the first in 1861-62, followed by others in 1863-64 and 1873-74.

Australia's first (white team) to England in turn was in 1878 but it was only in 1880 at the Oval that they played what came to be recorded as the first official Test match on English soil. And two years later at the same venue was born 'The Ashes', symbol of supremacy in Anglo-Australian Test cricket ever since, following Australia's gripping seven-run win. In 1889 South Africa became the third Test playing nation.

Lord Harris in 1878-79 took the second English team to Australia for a Test match and reciprocal visits continued through the 1880s, team braving arduous and often-times dangerous sea voyages that lasted more than two months.

The first five-Test series was staged in Australia in 1884-85 with the fight for the Ashes adding extra spice to the contests.

The new decade began with England in Australia in 1891-92. The tour was sponsored by Lord Sheffield in whose name Australia's domestic trophy the Sheffield Shield was instituted (thanks to a grant of 150 Pounds Sterling) and Australia returned to the 'mother country' in 1893.

It should be noted that all the English cricket teams visit to Australia in the 19th century were possible only due to funding by private companies, including the very first in 1861-62 which was bankrolled by two England-born Melbourne-based caterers, Messrs Christopher Pond and Felix William Spiers who thus preceded Australian business tycoon Kerry Packer and his short-lived World Series Cricket by more than a century.

But despite some memorable matches, interest in Test cricket was beginning to flag in both England and Australia. Wrote famed historian David Frith: "What cricket now needed at a top level was a Test series on a spectacular scale, to assert the Anglo-Australian bond and to establish once and for all the primacy of Test cricket which was so slow in establishing itself." *(Stoddy's Mission: The First Great Test Series 1894-95; page 12)*

The plans to bring the English cricketers to Australia in 1893-94 were thrown into jeopardy by the refusal of the massively wealthy and cricket mad Lord Sheffield (1832-1909) to sponsor the tour as he had done with the previous one in 1891-92 which despite the presence of WG Grace had made a loss of 2,000 Pounds Sterling.

This is where Parsee cricketer MD Kanga, a member of the 1888 team to England, comes into the picture.

Kanga was on a visit to Australia and met with former Test cricketer Harry Boyle in Melbourne. They discussed the prospect of bringing a team of Parsee cricketers to Australia in 1893-94 as Lord Sheffield "had abandoned the idea of bringing a team of English cricketers to Australia in 1893-94" as per a report in *The Australian Star* daily dated July 27, 1893.

It is obvious news of the Parsees' historic wins over both the first two English teams to visit India, GF Vernon's XI in 1889-90 and Lord Hawke's in 1892-93, had spread far and wide and they now found themselves in demand.

A report in the *Evening Journal* of Adelaide (July 17, 1893) also mentions the proposed tour and notes that Lord Hawke who brought a "fairly strong amateur 11 out to India" lost just two of their 23 matches including one to the Parsees. So these wins were making waves around the cricket world.

Boyle had been appointed as agent for the proposed tour by Kanga and the July 27 report further states that though time was short, "Mr. Kanga thinks there is every possibility of the tour being satisfactorily arranged."

The *Evening Journal* quoted Kanga as saying that Framjee Patel, who was instrumental in organizing the first tour of England in 1886 would also help in organising the Australian visit.

However, just six months later, the proposed tour stood cancelled, a report in *The Capricornian* daily dated January 13, 1894 stating: "The Australasian Cricket Council decided not to grant their patronage to a Parsee cricket team's visit pending the probable visit of an English team."

After Lord Sheffield declined, the Melbourne Cricket Club and the trustees of the Sydney Cricket Ground combined to finance the 1894-95 tour which proved to be a tremendous success financially, garnering a substantial profit of 7,000 Pounds with crowds flocking to every match. Within days of the *The Capricornian* report of the Parsee cancellation, the backers of the tour approached AE Stoddart as the England captain to raise a side for the tour.

According to Frith: "The five Test matches were reported as never before, the narrative compelling, thanks to the long chain of incident and the colourful nature of the players who made it. *The Pall Mall Gazette* broke new ground by publishing—at riskily high expense—long cabled reports from the other side of the world, close on the heels of the action…Even Queen Victoria, not renowned for her interest in cricket, became curious as the public excitement rose, and demanded to be kept up to date on the 1894-95 battle for the Ashes."

The series swung back and forth dramatically, gripping both countries. England won the first two Test matches, Australia the next two to draw level before Stoddart's men clinched the fifth and final by six wickets at Melbourne to keep the Ashes.

This was just the shot in the arm that Test cricket and the Ashes needed. Cricket would never be the same again.

But **what if** the late sponsorship had not come through for the Ashes and the Parsees had instead toured Australia? Would Test cricket have withered on the vine and faded away?

Food for thought!

CHAPTER TWO

Indian Captaincy's Royal Roundabout

Vizzy's Machinations Lead the Way

Before India's mega-rich businessmen and India's movie superstars, before corporate sponsorship, before even government—mainly bank—jobs, there was Indian royalty.

As Indian cricket took off in the 1920s with the wildly popular Quadrangular tournament and the path-breaking visit of the first MCC team to India in 1926-27, it was India's multitude of maharajas, princes, nawabs and wannabe royalty that stepped in to bankroll cricket in India.

Just as the owners of the Indian Premier League (IPL) franchises flaunt their star players in ego battles against fellow-owners, so too royalty back then indulged in one-upmanship against fellow- royals.

Indian cricket fans as a result were blessed to watch all-time legends of the game brought out at great expense to augment teams floated by the royals.

The biggest names in world cricket made fleeting appearances on Indian soil, including England's Harold Larwood, George Hirst, Wilfred Rhodes, CB Fry, Jack Hobbs and Herbert Sutcliffe plus West

Indian fast bowling all-rounder Learie (later, Lord Learie) Constantine, the first cricket superstar from the Caribbean—all part of the ego battles between Indian royalty for whom cricket was a vehicle for vanity, prestige and a way to suck up to the ruling British Raj.

Further, all the leading Indians too were employed by the princes who gave them grandiose titles like Colonel (CK Nayudu) and Captain (Vijay Hazare).

Even as the IPL franchise owners nearly a century later demanded and got their pound of flesh, so too Indian royalty extracted a price for their largesse. And the biggest prize of all was the captaincy of the Indian national team.

The old saying—one of my personal favourites—that there is nothing new in cricket was thus proven correct once again.

By the 1890s the Hindu and Muslim communities were picking up the gauntlet from the Parsees and enthusiastically taking to the game.

After the Oxford University Authentics team of 1902-03 became the first tourists to play against Hindu and Muslim sides, the idea was hatched by the canny JM Framjee Patel—the 19th century Parsee Kerry Packer—to take a combined team to England, dubbed 'All-India'. This would include players from all the religious communities, hence giving it an authentic pan-India look.

The plan failed to take off due to the fierce rivalry between Parsees, Hindus and Muslims as to the composition of the team, though lack of finances was the official reason given in January 1904 when it was finally called off.

In fact, this was not Patel's first attempt. Between 1897 to 1900 he worked feverishly to fulfill his cherished goal. His dream was to have the first prince of cricket, Kumar Shri Ranjitsinhji, one of the immortals of cricket who had represented England in Tests with distinction, to lead the Indian side. But Ranji did not want to jeopardize his England career, and his refusal to lead the All-India team also meant the financial backing for the visit never materialized.

After the second failed attempt, for which Ranji's public contempt for the team's chances in England was also a dampener, fresh impetus to the tour was given by violent acts against the British rulers and their local collaborators between 1907 and 1909. This dismayed the Indian loyalists, particularly the princes and now the idea for the tour was pushed forward by their desire to project their loyalty to the crown.

The background to the tour and the political and sporting implications have been brilliantly laid out by Prashant Kidambi in his 2019 book *Cricket Country: The Untold History of the First All India Team.*

This was the first occasion when Indian royalty stamped its influence on local cricket in an authoritative manner. For the captain of the team was none other than the 19-year-old Maharaja Bhupendra Singh of the fabulously wealthy and powerful House of Patiala, whose sway over Indian cricket would continue till independence.

This time with the House of Tata's full backing, there was no excuse of paucity of funds. Patel's tireless efforts to take an All-India team to England finally paid off after years of efforts. Kidambi's outstanding research busts the myth that Patiala had anything to do with the organization of the tour, save for a financial contribution.

The team was announced in Bombay on March 1, 1911, and though the selection of Bhupendra as captain came as a surprise, the Maharaja was no mean cricketer. The 16-member team consisted of seven Parsees, as well as Hindus, Muslims and the Sikh captain.

Bhupendra's short reign had been a troubled one till then with rumours of drunken debauchery being deeply concerning for his English masters. They approved his trip as it was felt it would be good for him to be away from the intrigues of the Patiala court.

Further, the year marked the coronation of King George V and as one of the foremost royals in Britain's 'Jewel in the crown', the Maharaja of Patiala's presence at the occasion was seen as diplomatically vital.

London was bursting at the seams with heads of state and royalty from around the world flocking to the capital. The ceremonies, pageantry and parades lasted the whole summer.

Bhupendra as one of the most prominent royals thus spent most of the tour outside the cricket field. Indeed, he played in only three of the 14 matches even though he was one of the leading batsmen. In those three games, including the most prestigious, against MCC at Lord's, he had scores of 47, 6, 0, 10 (the latter two v MCC), 16 and 28, thus finishing his truncated portion of the tour with 107 runs from six innings at the average of 17.83.

The leading player in the team was Kekhashru Maneksha Mistry, a famous all-rounder who was one of the foremost Parsee cricketers of his age.

Unfortunately for All-India, he was also the Maharaja's *aide-de-camp*, right-hand man and legal guardian appointed by the Maharaja's late father. In this capacity he was indispensable for the Maharaja's official functions of which there were countless including a private audience with the newly crowned king, a rare privilege.

The side was thus crippled without its two leading players and this was reflected in the disastrous results—played 14, won two, lost ten, drawn two. Mistry topped the averages, but like his ruler played just three matches. His highest score of 78 was the only bright spot in their innings rout at the hands of MCC. Surely if he had been allowed to play more matches the results would have been better. But it was not to be, and *Wisden* in its 1912 edition was scathing in its criticism.

The fallout was that Indian cricket rather than progressing in its bid to gain world recognition took a giant step back.

The Imperial Cricket Conference (later International Cricket Council) was founded in 1909 with only three countries enjoying Test status, South Africa being the youngest. Whatever hopes India may have harboured of entering this exclusive club suffered a serious setback in 1911. This after all was one of the major reasons for Framjee Patel organizing the tour—the burning desire for India to be granted Test status alongside the Big Three of world cricket.

It would be a long wait for India's first official Test match at Lord's in 1932 though India were admitted to the ICC in 1926. Sadly the man who strove all his adult life to bring Indian cricket onto the world stage, Framjee Patel, was not around to witness the historic occasion as he passed away in October 1918.

But **what if** Bhupendra and Mistry had been available throughout the tour, enhancing the success rate of the team and enabling India to gain Test status in the 1920s rather than the 1930s?

A number of Indian cricketers were at their peak in that decade, some not making it to the Test side a decade later. It took India 20 years (they had no Tests between 1936 and 1946) and 25 matches to record their first win which came against England at Madras in 1952. It could well have come earlier if Test status had been granted in the 1920s.

While three teams from England toured India between GF Vernon's of 1892-93 and the Oxford University Authentics of 1902-03, there was a long gap of 15 years between the dismal All-India tour of England in 1911 and the visit of Arthur Gilligan's MCC in 1926-27, thereby setting Indian cricket back by at least a decade.

The middle-order batsman from Poona, DB Deodhar was already 34 when he scored 148 in the first unofficial Test at Bombay against MCC in December 1926. But at 40 he was deemed past his best when the first official team to tour England was selected six years later.

Deodhar's 148 was overshadowed just a fortnight earlier by CK Nayudu's barnstorming 153 for the Hindus which included 13 fours and 11 sixes, a world record at the time. That dazzling display which had the Bombay crowd in raptures is credited with being the moment when Gilligan realized that India deserved Test status.

Wisden in its reports on the tour clearly brought out the contrasts between the "dazzling display" of Nayudu's 153 in just over 100 minutes and Deodhar's "admirable defence during a stay of four hours and a quarter" for his 148. The two batting together in a Test match would have complemented each other perfectly. But alas, that was never to be.

Nayudu, who through a series of fortuitous circumstances would captain India in that maiden Test, was 38 when he made this debut at Lord's along with the ten other Indians in the team.

But although he had an outstanding tour and became the first Indian Test player to be chosen as one of *Wisden's* Five Cricketers of the Year in their 1933 edition, Nayudu was at peak form and fitness the decade earlier. One can only imagine what feats he might have achieved on the Test stage at the pinnacle of his powers. As it is, his Test average of 25 over just seven Tests does not do enough justice to his amazing talent.

Test opening bower L. Amar Singh's elder brother L. Ramji was a tearaway fast bowler who terrorized batsmen in the 1920s, including Gilligan's men. Born in 1900 he was way past his prime by the time he played in his lone Test in Bombay in December 1933.

It was Gilligan who took it upon himself to convince Indian officials to form the Board of Control for Cricket in India and then strongly recommend Test status for India to the ICC. But it could have all come earlier.

If only, if only…!

Enter Vizzy

At the start of this chapter I touched on the ego battles between India's royals for control of Indian cricket.

Edward Docker summed up their attitude succinctly in his 1976 book *History of Indian Cricket*: "Indian cricket would have been very dull without the glamour the princes brought to the game. Yet, at their worst, they could be impossible; like spoiled children they quarreled, sulked and were insanely jealous of one another."

And right through the 1930s, until his untimely death in 1938 aged 46, it was Bhupendra Singh, the Maharaja of Patiala and Vijayananda Gajapathi Raju, the Maharajkumar of Vizianagaram, better known as Vizzy—a small-time royal-cum-*zamindar* (land-owner) with a big-time ego—who had Indian cricket in a tizzy with their tit-for-tat battles.

The shenanigans over captaincy of the three touring teams to England in 1932, 1936 and 1946 made a mockery of the nascent Test nation with the princes playing a toxic role.

For the maiden tour the names in the hat were all of royal stock—Prince Duleepsinhji (nephew of Ranji) who had already played for England; Iftikhar Ali Khan, the Nawab of Pataudi (senior) who was on the cusp of doing so; and inevitably, Bhupendra Singh of Patiala. Also, lurking and sulking in the background was Vizzy who of all these candidates was the only one with no cricket (and little royal) pedigree. The selectors even briefly considered England captain Douglas Jardine as he was born in Bombay. Jardine was already captain of England so this idea was rather fanciful, even though West Indies cricket for the first four decades was always led by white men. However, Jardine, Duleep and Pataudi all declined—but I am not going into any fanciful **what if?** scenarios around the future Bodyline captain!

Pataudi though was a strong a contender and withdrew at the eleventh hour even after leading in some of the trial matches in India, apparently concerned his qualifications for English county Worcestershire would be in jeopardy.

Initially Patiala was announced as captain, with Prince Ghanshyamsinhji Limbdi as his vice-captain and the comically named 'Deputy Vice-Captain' post going to the disgruntled Vizzy who declined in protest. Patiala it was already known was too busy with his princely functions and also withdrew.

Limbdi remained as vice-captain and a new captain, his brother-in-law Maharaja of Porbandar (Natwarsinhji Bhavsinhji) was appointed, who like Vizzy was a nonentity as a cricketer.

With Porbandar sensibly declining to lead at Lord's considering his miserable form on tour (scores of 0, 0 and 2, leading to the jibe that he was the only cricketer to own more Rolls-Royces than score runs on a tour of England) and Limbdi being unfit, Nayudu eventually got to lead as practically the fourth, but best choice as captain.

But **what if** either Porbandar or Limbdi had captained at Lord's? It would surely have made a mockery of Indian Test cricket at its very birth. For despite expectedly losing the lone Test, the babes of Test cricket were far from disgraced and for that the leadership skills of Nayudu must be lauded.

Vizzy got his way four years later though. He grabbed the captaincy with both hands after a tour of India that reeked of a US Presidential election, promising support, largesse and team places right and left if he got their votes.

Pataudi was once again a leading candidate, but this time withdrew in disgust at Vizzy's politicking. His *coup de grace* was toadying up to the cricket-crazy Viceroy Lord Willingdon, funding the pavilion at Delhi's Ferozeshah Kotla named after him (and to this day remains the Willingdon Pavilion) and donating the Willingdon Gold Cup Trophy.

The Viceroy allegedly pressured Pataudi to withdraw his candidacy which should have been a shoo-in such were the Nawab's skills as a batsman and leader at the zenith of his powers.

For Vizzy it was the culmination of a ten-year dream for which he had spent enormous time, money, energy and resources. But for Indian cricket in general and star all-rounder Lala Amarnath in particular it would be a nightmare that every genuine cricket lover wished they could have woken up from.

Between 1933 and 1936, India played twice at home, one official (three Tests v Douglas Jardine's England/MCC side) and one unofficial (four 'Tests' v Jack Ryder's Australian team).

Ryder's team was bankrolled by Bhupendra with the stated idea of preparing the Indian team for the 1936 England tour. As always with the princes there was an ulterior motive, in this case his plot to appoint his son Yadavendrasingh, the Yuvraj of Patiala as captain in 1936.

Nayudu was captain in the home Test series v England but things got complicated when the Australians toured India for the first time. Yadavendra, who played a lone Test in his career against England at Madras in February 1934, doing well in scoring 24 and 60, captained in the first unofficial Test at Bombay. But this led to a public outcry at this act of nepotism and he was replaced as captain by Nayudu for the second at Calcutta. But then dirty politics saw to it that Nayudu was replaced by Syed Wazir Ali for the next two Tests.

Doomed from the Start

The 1936 tour was doomed from the start. Though the party consisted of 17 players, others came and went, some undeserved, in order to reward those state associations who had backed Vizzy. In all 22 players took part in the matches on tour, causing confusion and resentment in the ranks. The touring party was split into two camps, the Nayudu camp—largely made up of those owning allegiance to Bhupendra, and the Vizzy camp, the captain being the sworn enemy of Bhupendra.

Amarnath was in the employ of the House of Patiala and naturally felt intense loyalty to the Maharaja. But Viceroy Willingdon, who had a toxic influence over Indian cricket was implacably opposed to Bhupendra

Further, Amarnath was a protégé of Nayudu, his first captain and this proved a double whammy against the young superstar of Indian cricket. He had captured the imagination of the nation and the cricket world by becoming the first Indian to score a Test century, that too on debut against England in Bombay in December 1933.

Vizzy was intensely jealous of the massive fan following, star status and dazzling cricket skills of both Nayudu and Amarnath and did everything to humiliate and insult them and their friends on the miserable tour. Unlike the Maharaja of Porbandar who had the modesty and good sense to step down from the captaincy on the previous tour, Vizzy had no such plans— despite a request from leading batsman Vijay Merchant to do so before the start of the Test series and allow Nayudu to lead in his stead.

Lacking basic captaincy nous Vizzy infuriated his bowlers by not being capable of setting proper fields for them and his batsmen by constantly chopping and changing the batting order at his whim and fancy.

With a target painted on his back and with Vizzy provoking him from the start of the tour, it was only a matter of time before the short fuse of the hot-headed Punjabi lad lit up into a conflagration.

Rajender Amarnath in the 2004 biography of his father devotes a full chapter of 38 pages—the longest in the book—to the incident that shook Indian cricket and indeed Indian society to its core. (*The Making of a Legend: Lala Amarnath: Life and Times*; Chapter Three: 'Sent Home From Tour of England').

The bickering between the captain and one of his star players was a recurring theme from the start and came to a head in the match against Minor Counties at Lord's played between June 17 to 19, with the first Test at Lord's just a week away and only one warm-up game remaining.

Amarnath had been in brilliant form, both batting and bowling but had injury problems, which Vizzy and manager Captain Jack Brittain-Jones were most unsympathetic about. A staunch Establishment man with a strong streak of racism, he held the post of Comptroller of the Viceroy's Household. Both Vizzy the quisling and Brittain-Jones practised to perfection the notorious British policy of divide-and-rule.

Told to pad up by his captain, Amarnath was left stewing while one batsman after another was sent in before him. Finally with just ten minutes to stumps he was sent in at number seven and stormed back livid at the humiliating treatment. Throwing off his equipment, the not out batsman cursed loudly in his native Punjabi, which was duly translated for Vizzy and the manager.

Furious confrontations followed and the end result was Amarnath being sent home on disciplinary grounds. Though hectic parleys followed in a bid to bring him back in time for the second Test at Old Trafford—the first ended in a crushing defeat by nine wickets for the thoroughly demoralized Indians—it all came to naught.

It transpired that Vizzy had softened his stand on receiving apologies from a chastened Amarnath. But the manager with backing from the British government was determined to show to the world that Indians lacked the discipline to run their own cricket team, much less their own country. This came at a time when demands for Indian independence had reached boiling point.

However, the crisis would not have reached this shocking stage in the first place if Vizzy's quixotic ways and utter lack of competence on the field had been checked by agreeing to step down in favour of Nayudu.

So **what if** Amarnath had not been punished so harshly for his outburst and been allowed to stay on, how would that have affected the series India lost 2-0?

One can only go by his figures at the time of his untimely departure. In a word, they were outstanding. With 613 runs from 20 innings (average 32.26) he was the leading run-scorer for the team and in addition had 32 wickets at 20.87.

These figures would place him fourth in batting and first in bowling when the tour ended. Against Essex he became the first Indian to score a century in both innings on English soil (130 and 107 as well as six wickets in the match) and there was in addition an unbeaten 114 v Northamptonshire. His best bowling figures were 6 for 29 in the first innings against Middlesex at Lord's. Astonishingly, despite niggling injuries that required rest, he had played in every one of the first 12 matches.

Amarnath's bowling style was ideally suited to English pitch and weather conditions. Bowling off and leg cutters off the wrong foot at medium pace, even ten years later on the tour of 1946 he bowled brilliantly with five-wicket hauls in both the first Test at Lord's and second at Old Trafford.

At Lord's he sliced through the top of England's batting leaving the home side reeling at 70 for 4 as he scalped the big guns, Len Hutton, Cyril Washbrook, Denis Compton and Wally Hammond. And this when he was not at the peak of his powers! What wonders he could have done ten years earlier when at his peak? Indian cricket lovers can only look back with anguish at the shocking chain of events that deprived the touring team of his priceless services.

The 1936 tour was a dismal failure—played 31, won 5, lost 13, drew 13. Vizzy's career fortunately for one and all ended with the three Tests of 1936 and scores of 19, 6, 6, 0, 1 and 1.

So **what if** Pataudi had been captain instead of Vizzy?

This was asked of dashing opening batsman Mushtaq Ali exactly fifty years later:

Q. What do you think would have been the team spirit if Pataudi senior had gone as captain?

A: Very much better. We all knew what a class of cricketer he was. He had represented England and in those days for an Indian to play for England was something great.

(Interview by Andy O'Brien in *Sportsworld* dated July 23- 29, 1986; 'Living for Memories')

Pataudi Takes Over

Ten years later Pataudi finally got his chance. India were the first country to tour England post World War Two and for the third time in a row, following 1932 and 1936 it was a prince at the helm in England.

In the words of Mihir Bose in *The History of Indian Cricket* (page 60): "Like Banquo's ghost, Pataudi would cast a shadow over Indian cricket for some years…"

This peculiar situation had been going on since the early 1930s. Now political currents pushed the Nawab to the foreground. Of course nothing was straightforward in Indian cricket back then. And there were plenty of twists and turns in the run-up to the announcement of captain——political, cricket-related and even a combination of the two.

So why was Pataudi chosen to lead and not Vijay Merchant who was the popular and expected choice?

Merchant was in peak batting form while leading Bombay in the Ranji Trophy and also in the three unofficial Tests in 1945-46 against the visiting Australian Services team led by Lindsay Hassett. India won the third and final unofficial Test at Madras to take the series 1-0, the first time a foreign team had been beaten in a series in India.

But two incidents, which upset Board officials, may have weighed against him. In the first unofficial Test at Bombay the Aussies were left the impossible task of scoring 113 runs in just 20 minutes.

Needlessly Merchant placed eight fielders round the boundary and instructed his bowlers to bowl a negative line outside the stumps. This was seen as a contravention of the spirit of cricket and an enraged Prince Duleepsinhji (chairman of the selectors) in the pavilion railed at Merchant as he led the team back in: "Merchant, you have brought shame upon Indian cricket."

This was in December 1945, and doubts were being raised about Merchant's ultra-defensive style of captaincy which eschewed even the slightest of risks in ensuring the team did not lose.

The other incident occurred during the Ranji Trophy final between Bombay and Holkar at the Brabourne Stadium in March 1945.

Watching on was President of the BCCI and senior Congress politician Dr. Subbaroyan. He was shocked at some of the lbw decisions that he felt favoured Bombay and over-stepped his boundaries, berating the umpire and Bombay captain Merchant. Furious at the interference, Merchant ordered him out of the dressing-room.

A campaign was also brewing among the other state associations to curtail the powers of Bombay cricket which they felt was overpowering the rest of Indian cricket. The resentment was simmering on a slow boil and by 1943-44 the end of the hugely popular Pentangular tournament held before massive crowds was the first move to push back on Bombay's alleged hegemony. The campaign to scrap the communal tournament was led by Mahatma Gandhi and avidly backed outside Bombay cricket circles. Merchant led the chorus of protests from Bombay at its scrapping.

From now on the Ranji Trophy for the national championship launched in 1934-35 would be India's premier tournament.

Pataudi did a *volte face* of his own. Having previously praised the Pentangular, his speech in Poona in 1944 claiming he had stayed away from Indian cricket due to the communal nature of the tournament was contradictory to his long-held views. This was an early indication he was placing himself squarely in the anti-Bombay lobby.

Pataudi, whose first-class career began in England in 1928, had never played a first-class match on Indian soil, only a handful of exhibition games. But in February 1944 he captained Western States against Rest of India, his first first-class match since a county game for Worcestershire in 1938. That though flew under the radar, being of little consequence.

It was when he turned out for Southern Punjab against Delhi in the Ranji Trophy at Patiala in January 1946 that the cricket media and public stood up and took notice since it was just prior to the announcement of the captain for the 1946 tour of England.

The political angle involved Pataudi's father-in-law the Nawab of Bhopal. Even as the selection committee was meeting in Madras in January 1946, the Chamber of Princes was meeting in Delhi with Bhopal the Chancellor. With the country on the boil the pro-British princes were getting jittery as to what their fate would be with the new Labour government veering towards independence for India. Bhopal led the call for Dominion status for the princely states and having his princely son captain the nation in England would be a boon for them.

Bombay Ambushed!

The annual meeting in Madras has gone down in Indian cricket history as the Mad Hatter's Tea Party. Chaos ensued, Bombay were ambushed and to their shock and dismay, Pataudi was voted captain by a narrow 10-8 margin against Merchant.

Some members of the 1946 team, Vijay Hazare and Mushtaq Ali in particular, expressed their outrage in books released years later.

Hazare wrote in his 1981 autobiography *A Long Innings*: "He [Merchant] was the victim of the power-politics in Indian cricket and was by-passed for the honour…Pataudi, with all his past standing was not an active cricketer in India. Many knew him only by his one-time reputation. He did not appear to be in the best of health…"

In fact it was due to his poor health that Pataudi only played a handful of matches between the 1935 and 1938 county seasons for Worcestershire.

The first health scare had flared up in 1931 during the-then highly prestigious Varsity match between Oxford University and Cambridge at Lord's. Cambridge batting first scored 385 with Alan Ratcliffe's 201 being a new record for the fixture. Overnight the young Nawab promised his team-mates he would surpass the record for Oxford and that is just what he did with a brilliant innings of 238 not out to take his team to victory.

But the strain of batting for five hours proved almost fatal as he collapsed in the dressing room. There are conflicting reports over the place and nature of the collapse but it was an open secret in English cricket circles that the Nawab had heart issues.

The 1946 tour lasted over four months with a total of 33 matches including the three Tests—hard to believe in this day and age of drastically truncated tours. The captain played 20 of those games, including the Test series which must have put an immense strain on his health considering he had played just eight first-class matches between 1935 to the start of the tour in May 1946, obviously on doctor's orders.

It was his father-in-law Hafiz Muhammad Hamidullah Khan Bahadur, the Nawab of Bhopal, who was reportedly behind his decision to tour and which Iftikhar obeyed like a loyal son-in-law. But **what if** he had declined on doctor's orders?

In a tragic turn of events Pataudi's heart gave out at the young age of 41 while playing polo in Delhi in 1951 on what happened to be his son's 11th birthday. He had so much more to give to his family and to the newly independent nation in which he had decided to stay on while one of his sisters moved to Pakistan. And he could have served India in different capacities both politically where he had much experience as well as in cricket matters.

And what of Merchant, whose dream of captaining India in official Tests would once again be shattered, this time on health grounds, for the next tour, Australia in 1947-48?

One of India's greatest batsmen took it stoically. He served as Pataudi's loyal lieutenant, playing in 30 of the 33 matches and captaining in all the games in his captain's absence, becoming the first and only Indian to score over 2,000 runs on a tour. Pataudi though was a failure in the Tests. England won the series 1-0.

Most, if not all the team members felt it was only just if Merchant had been chosen as captain.

Wrote Mushtaq in his 1976 autobiography *Cricket Delightful* (page 178): "What I did not like about it was the selection of Nawab of Pataudi as captain. But I shall unhesitatingly state he made a fine job of it."

But did he? And **what if** Merchant had been made captain instead?

A letter from Mushtaq Ali to his mentor Nayudu from Taunton, Somerset, dated 1 August 1946 lays bare Pataudi's inadequacies and the disquiet within the team.

The letter was published in its original form in *The Illustrated History of Indian Cricket* by Boria Majumdar (pages 84-85) under the headline 'Every Man for Himself.'

"In my humble opinion the tour is worst *[sic]* than 1936, the same old trouble; no team work at all. Every member of the team is for himself. No one cares for the country at all. Amarnath is the cause of all these things; then Pataudi [who] is very much a changed man over here, he is very much against the Indian players… As a captain he is worse than a schoolboy…I am very much fed up with him as are the other members of the Indian team…I think Merchant is a much better captain than this fellow."

Berry Sarbadhadikary wrote in the inaugural edition of *Indian Cricket Almanack* for 1946-47: "I can personally vouch for the fact that the team pulled together as well as, shall we say, Oxford had rowed from Putney to Mortlake that year." [He was referring to the Boat Race won by Oxford in 1946].

That a tight lid was kept on the rumblings within the team against the captain was perhaps due to the able manager Pankaj Gupta and vice-captain Merchant who did not allow his bitter disappointment to get the better of him.

At least not in 1946. But the simmering anger and resentment within Merchant at the perceived injustice in being bypassed manifested itself in a stunning incident that rocked Indian cricket 25 years later in one of the biggest **what if** moments of them all, as we shall see later in the book.

CHAPTER THREE

Going Down Under

The Missing Four M's and The Don

Bradman's Invincibles. The very name evokes shock—among its opponents—and awe among cricket fans worldwide.

In three post-war series of five Tests each the team from 1946 to 1948 did not lose a single Test, winning 3-0, 4-0 and 4-0; that's 11 out of 15 Tests including six by an innings and the others by huge margins too.

Any team with Sir Donald Bradman in it would be well-nigh invincible but the Australian team of that period was packed with master batsmen, superb fast bowlers and brilliant all-rounders—an unbeatable combination.

This then was the daunting task for Lala Amarnath and his men as they became the first cricket team to fly to their destination rather than take the long and arduous sea voyage.

The Indian team had toured England three times, in 1932, 1936 and 1946 but not visited any of the other Test playing nations. In addition, it had hosted only England in 1933-34 for an official Test series. And for the first time it was faced with the challenge of a full-fledged five—Test series.

Lindsay Hassett had brought an Australian Services team to India in 1945-46, just a couple of months after it had played a series of 'Victory Tests' in England to celebrate the victory of the Allies in World War Two (1939-45).

Hassett's team, which had a young Keith Miller in it, played three unofficial Tests in India, losing the series 1-0. It was the first time India had won an unofficial Test series—it was yet to record a single official Test win, losing six and drawing the other four, all against England. And it was Hassett who reported back to the Australian authorities that India were worthy of a full-fledged tour.

The third Indian tour of England in 1946 was the most successful of the three. India lost the series 1-0 but acquitted itself well in the county matches.

Historic Series

This was the background to what would be a historic series for the Indian cricket team. But the timing of the series, decided more than 12 months previously could not have been worse.

The British announced they would be leaving India after centuries of colonial rule. India would be divided, the new nation of Pakistan being born (or torn) out of it.

What followed was the displacement of millions of Hindus and Sikhs from what would be Pakistan and of Muslims in India fleeing to the new nation. This was accompanied by bloody riots with massive casualties on both sides and the departing British washing their hands off the disaster and tragedy.

Indian gained her independence on 15 August 1947, Pakistan its birth one day earlier. But the joy of freedom was overshadowed by the horrific bloodshed.

In the midst of all this turmoil the Indian board's challenge was to carve the first team out of independent India. No longer would it be called 'All-India'. Of course this challenge was nothing compared to that faced by the governments of both nations.

Nonetheless, a team had to be chosen and sent to Australia if international sporting commitments were to be honoured. And the first role to be decided was that of the captain, India's premier opening batsmen and one of the finest in the world, Vijay Merchant who had covered himself with glory on both the 1936 and 1946 England tours (see previous chapter).

For Merchant it was the culmination of a long-cherished desire, something that was cruelly thwarted by the selection of Iftikhar Ali Khan Pataudi (sr) as captain in England in 1946.

Merchant's vice-captain was the brilliant all-rounder Lala Amarnath who though not fulfilling the early batting promise of a century on debut in 1933 was nonetheless a vital cog in the brains-trust of any Indian team and a canny medium pace bowler to boot.

So for the first time royalty was not the first choice as leader of an Indian touring team as had been the case on the three tours of England. It was a significant landmark for the newly independent nation.

Merchant was joined by his favourite opening partner, Mushtaq Ali, he of the dazzling (and some said irresponsible) strokes and dashing personality, a worthy successor to his mentor CK Nayudu

Merchant and Mushtaq, as contrasting an opening pair as Sunil Gavaskar and K. Srikkanth in the 1980s, gave India tremendous starts with three-figure stands both in the 1936 and 1946 series, a formidable world-class pair at the top of the batting order.

The batting was strengthened lower down the order by Rusi Modi, the first Indian to score 1,000-plus runs in a Ranji Trophy season, all silken grace, and the ever-improving Vijay Hazare whose appetite for runs in domestic cricket would soon be matched at the international level. Both made excellent debuts in the first Test at Lord's in 1946 just as Sourav Ganguly and Rahul Dravid did at the same venue exactly 50 years later.

Fazal Mahmood was unfortunate to miss out on selection for England, thought by the selectors to be too young and raw. Now was his chance to open the bowling, his cut and seam at a fair pace reminiscent of the bowling style of England's master medium pace swing bowler Alec Bedser.

Another youngster, the promising all-rounder Dattu Phadkar, plus Amarnath made up a decent opening bowling trio.

Vinoo Mankad on his maiden tour of England had become the first and only Indian to perform the double of 1,000 runs and 100 wickets on a tour. He had emerged as the leading left-arm spinner in the world and one of the leading all-rounders, challenged only by Australia's dynamic fast bowling all-rounder Keith Miller.

The Team

The team was announced as early as 17 March 1947 when the partition of the country had yet to be decided. It was a full seven months before the commencement of the tour with a four-day game against Western Australia at Perth starting October 17, the squad expected to land Down Under on October 11.

Despite the political uncertainty the BCCI decided to go ahead and choose the team. Even five months before the fateful dates of August 14 and 15 no one in India or Britain knew what events would unfold over the next few months, such was the chaos and lack of planning by the British. Indeed Board President AS De Mello announced the team with the map of undivided India behind him. Whether it was an act of bravado, innocence or naivety is hard to tell.

The team was: Vijay Merchant (captain), Lala Amarnath (vice-captain), Hemu Adhikari, Mushtaq Ali, Amir Elahi, Vijay Hazare, Jamshed Irani, Gogumal Kishenchand, Vinoo Mankad, Fazal Mahmood, Rusi Modi, CS Nayudu, Dattu Phadkar, Khandu Rangnekar, Probir Sen and Ranga Sohoni.

It was the famous 18th century Scottish poet Robert Burns who coined the phrase "the best laid plans of mice and men go awry."

It is not known if Burns was a follower of cricket but this phrase would have been ringing in the ears of De Mello and co. assuming they had heard of it.

One by one they fell like dominoes—the captain-designate and ace opener Vijay Merchant, middle order batsman Rusi Modi, promising pace bowler Fazal Mahmood and star opener Mushtaq Ali.

Modi it was announced dropped out on medical grounds, though nothing more specific was forthcoming.

Kersi Meher-Homji in his 2018 book *From Bradman to Kohli: Best of India–Australia Test Cricket* wrote Rusi Modi had a "nervous breakdown."

However, according to what I was told by someone well connected with the team, the reason was Modi was to get married and so decided to skip the long tour. In fact England 1946 would be the first and only tour of his sadly curtailed Test career.

And what of Mushtaq Ali? In his column in *The Telegraph*, Kolkata ('Cricketing Might-Have-Beens'; 28 May 2005) which I cited in my introduction as one of the inspirations for this book, leading Indian cricket historian Ramachandra Guha wrote: "Mushtaq's family was caught in the communal conflagration of those horrible months before and after August 1947; he first backed out because of threats to his family and then, when things sort of settled down, said he would go, only to be told by the Indian Cricket Board they could not take him."

However this is not how Mushtaq tells it in his autobiography *Cricket Delightful* in the chapter 'Bowled Out'.

Mushtaq's explains it was the death of his eldest brother Iqbal that plunged the family into grief and turmoil.

Since the death of their father, Iqbal had assumed the role of head of the family. Now Mushtaq found himself thrust into the role.

"In such a predicament, I had no alternative but to send a wire to the Cricket Board President, Mr. Anthony de Mello, stating that because of my bereavement, I was unable to make the trip to Australia," wrote Mushtaq.

But once the mourning period was over the Holkar Maharaja, in whose employ Mushtaq was in, persuaded him to change his mind and send another telegram to De Mello informing him of the change in plans.

But to Mushtaq's dismay he was told it was too late for his inclusion, De Mello claiming the team had already been finalized, though Mushtaq claimed that no replacement for him had been announced at the time. A bitter Mushtaq lashed out at De Mello for what he perceived as a grave personal injustice.

In fact it was Fazal who got caught up in the partition violence, not Mushtaq.

He attended trial matches in Delhi in which he impressed and was selected as the youngest member of the touring party. The players were told to assemble at Poona for the training camp on August 15, that fateful and historic day. From Delhi Fazal returned to his hometown of Lahore where there was a curfew due to communal violence. Despite that he managed to reach Poona for the two-week camp which was abandoned due to persistent rain. The team was now told to assemble at Calcutta on October 9 to fly out to Australia.

From Poona he went to Bombay by train en-route to Lahore. CK Nayudu was travelling with him and saved him from two attackers by brandishing his bat and warning them off.

Horrified by the ferocity of the riots he had witnessed, Fazal decided against going to Australia. Amarnath, also from Lahore which he had to flee, tried to persuade the 22-year-old to change his mind, confident the talented bowler would be an asset on Australian pitches. But Fazal had by now made up his mind to stay in Lahore and ply his trade in Pakistan. All this was narrated in dramatic fashion in his 2003 autobiography *From Dawn to Dusk: Autobiography of a Pakistan Cricket Legend.*

India also lost the services of spinner/all-rounder Abdul Hafeez Kardar who had played all three Tests for India in England in 1946 and would become in 1952 the first captain of Pakistan in official Tests.

Merchant Drops Out

Merchant's case was the most long drawn out and his absence the most telling. Till the eleventh hour it appeared he would be fit for Australia.

Three months after the team had been announced, Merchant was lauded by the Maharaja of Porbander at the inauguration of a coaching school in Porbander.

The following extracts are from the full speeches published in a 1948 book titled *Cricket.*

"Here we have amongst us today our great captain Vijay Merchant who in a few months from now will be leading an All-India team in Australia..."

Merchant responded: "I can say very sincerely that the team given to me and under my care is one of the best that could have been chosen from the talent at our disposal."

But then amidst rising tension among Indian cricket followers, reports started trickling in regarding his worsening health.

On August 19 De Mello told the press that in the event of Merchant not being fit, the captaincy would pass to Amarnath. The captain-elect was given a deadline of September 5 to make a final call.

Right till the deadline there was hope Merchant would be declared fit. But it was not to be, an abdominal strain being the reason cited for his dropping out.

So the man who scored India's maiden Test century in 1933 and was three years later sent home from England under a cloud was now to lead free India's first national cricket team. Meanwhile, the man who led India in 16 unofficial Tests between 1937-38 and 1950-51 had his final hopes of captaining in an official Test dashed. No wonder Amarnath would always refer jokingly to Merchant as "India's unofficial Test captain!"

The selectors now had to hastily name replacements and they went for K. Rai Singh of Patiala, KS Ranvirsinhji of Jamnagar, Chandu Sarwate of Holkar and opening bowler CR Rangachari of Madras of whom only Sarwate had prior Test experience.

Rai Singh, Maharaja of Patialia's cousin and Ranvirsinhji, nephew of Ranji and cousin of Duleep were both a nod to Indian cricket's moth-eaten royal traditions. They were misfits in the touring team with Ranvir being the only member of the party not to play a single Test while Rai played the lone Test of his career in the third at Melbourne. Unfortunately the replacements including Sarwate were not a patch on the three stalwart batsmen and the one skilful pace bowler.

If all four of the original selected had been available, the XI for the opening Test at Brisbane starting on November 28 would probably have looked like this:

Openers: Vijay Merchant (captain) and Mushtaq Ali.

Middle order: Rusi Modi, Vijay Hazare, Lala Amarnath, Hemu Adhikari.

Wicket-keeper: Probir Sen/Jamshed Irani (they took it in turn to play the Tests).

Bowlers/all-rounders: Vinoo Mankad (spin), Dattu Phadkar (pace), CS Nayudu (spin) and Fazal Mahmood (pace) with Amarnath also bowling pace.

Instead it was: Mankad, Sarwate, Gul Mohammad, Adhikari, Kishenchand, Hazare, Amarnath, Rangnekar, Sohoni, Nayudu, Irani.

India were trounced in the Tests by an innings and 226 runs, 233 runs, an innings and 16 runs and an innings and 177 runs with the second Test at Sydney drawn on an even keel with rain preventing all but 10 hours of play over six days.

But **what if** the four M's had made the tour, how different would the result of the series have been?

In the words of Bradman in his 1950 autobiography *Farewell to Cricket:* "At the outset there was great disappointment when Merchant had to withdraw…There were other withdrawals, too, of prominent players which must have affected the overall strength of the team. But it was the loss of Merchant that I think was mainly responsible for India's relatively poor performance in the Test matches."

There is no doubt Australia was one of the most formidable teams of all time. Even without Bradman, who retired at the end of the 1948 series in England, they would continue their winning run.

Apart from Bradman, the batting had such legends as opener Arthur Morris, Sid Barnes, the teenage Neil Harvey and the veteran Lindsay Hassett. Wicket-keeper Don Tallon is considered one of the all-time greats and then there was one of the most fearsome opening bowling attacks of all time in Ray Lindwall and Keith Miller. Spin was a bit thin but Ian Johnson and Bill Johnston (who bowled both left arm pace and spin) were more than adequate.

India's strength was sapped, there can be no doubt. Hazare covered himself with glory becoming the first Indian batsman to score centuries in both innings of a Test; Phadkar was the big batting surprise, remarkably heading the Test averages and Mankad was at his all-round best. But only twice in the five Tests did the team cross 300 runs and with nine players making their debuts in the series, their inexperience was ruthlessly exposed.

What wonders the experienced opening pair of Merchant and Mushtaq could have achieved! So by my estimation Australia would still have won, but not by such a resounding margin—and maybe, just maybe with the edge given to the bowling by Fazal, India could even have sneaked in a win; one can dream, anyway!

India won just two of the 14 first-class matches on tour; one of them was notable for being against the 'Australian XI' at Sydney a fortnight before the first Test at Brisbane. Eight of the 11 in that team would feature in the Test series that was to follow including captain Bradman himself so it was virtually the Test team.

This was the match in which Bradman recorded the 100th first-class century of an amazing career at his favourite ground. But while the eyes of the cricket world were on the first non-Englishman to reach the landmark and in the fewest number of innings by far, the Indians pulled off a huge surprise winning the match by 47 runs.

Mankad had 10 wickets in the match including 8 for 84 in the second innings as the Australians went for the winning target of 251 runs in 150 minutes, but fell short.

The lack of bowling resources meant Amarnath had to bowl the second most number of overs in the series, second only to Mankad, while taking the most number of wickets in the process. But all that bowling sapped his energy and severely affected his batting with a highest score of just 46 in 10 Test innings.

Ironically outside the Test series he batted magnificently with five centuries including 228 against Victoria which contemporary reports described as one of the greatest innings played at the Melbourne Cricket Ground and topped both the tour runs aggregate and averages.

What if his bowlers had performed better, freeing him to concentrate on his batting? What a boon it would have been for the side.

Rain the Pain

But there was another crucial factor that fell heavily in favour of the hosts and this is where the normally shrewd Amarnath miscalculated.

The MCC norm at the time was to keep pitches uncovered, surprising since rain plays such a major role during the English summer. That was what Amarnath insisted on.

It was summer in the Southern Hemisphere and it turned out to be one of the wettest on record. Amarnath would not have known that nor of course would he have known that Bradman would win the toss four times out of five, more crucial than usual due to the weather and subsequent pitch conditions.

So when given the option before the start of the series he insisted the pitches should be uncovered, according to son Rajendar in his father's biography.

"It would be suicidal, he [Amarnath] felt, taking chances against the strength of the Australians. He knew the best chance was to catch the home side on wet wickets."

But just the opposite happened and it was India that found itself trapped over and over again on what the Aussies called a 'sticky dog.'

Let Bradman take up the story from his autobiography: "There had been correspondence between the Australian Board of Control and the Indian Board regarding the playing conditions in Australia. There were no differences of opinion excepting that Australia felt it would be more advantageous to the Indians if wickets were covered.

Surprisingly the Indians decided they would prefer the MCC idea of uncovered wickets.

I thought India was making a grave mistake. We do not see many wet wickets in this country, but we see more than the Indians do in theirs.

Our players do not possess quite the same skills as Englishmen under these conditions, but it seemed clear they would have more than the Indians.

I felt that we would prove superior on dry wickets. Knowing the merits of the players we would have at our disposal, I felt that on wet wickets the Indians would be overwhelmed.

For this I strongly pressed for the Indians to agree to covered wickets and spent considerable time trying to persuade Amarnath, the Indian Captain, of the soundness of my views. It was all to no avail.

I think probably Amarnath saw the wisdom of my suggestion, but was willing to trust the favouritism of the weather gods.

On the contrary the Indians suffered grievously through being caught on wet wickets. The result of the matches may not have been affected, though most certainly the end was expedited."

In fact three of the four matches which ended in defeat for the Indians did so before the final stipulated day, the first at Brisbane being the exception. The Australian authorities were anxious about this happening as it would affect ticket sales. Which is why they were so keen on the pitches being covered. Ultimately Amarnath's gamble backfired both on the team's chances and the finances of the tour. It would be 20 long years before another Indian team was invited to tour Australia.

Brisbane's 'Sticky Dog'

The weather and the toss, those two imponderables, struck at the Indians right at the start of the series at Brisbane.

"The result of the First Test Match was actually decided when the spin of the coin favoured Australia on the first day," wrote former Australian captain Victor Richardson in his book *Indian Cricketers in Australia 1947*.

Batting first Australia had reached 273 for three on a flat pitch when the rain came down and ended play early. Bradman was on a masterly 160 at stumps, going for quick runs with rain threatening even as the light worsened. He could have appealed against the light but declined. The Indians were impressed with his apparent dedication to play on. But Bradman knew the conditions intimately unlike the inexperienced Indians. He knew rain would eventually turn the pitch virtually unplayable due to Amarnath's refusal to have them covered and gamed the situation expertly, knowing full well batting in poor light was a better deal than on a gluepot of a pitch.

The weather on the second day saw almost the entire play ruined. But the crowd had grown restive and were demanding a refund. So the teams resumed at 5 pm with only an hour possible before Bradman this time successfully appealed against the light. The pitch was already proving difficult for batting and Bradman could only add 19 runs to progress from 160 to 179 while Australia eked out 36 runs, leaving them at 309 for three.

On the third morning with the pitch continuing to play tricks, Bradman was out hit wicket to Amarnath for 185. Never entirely comfortable in such conditions, the master was hit on the shoulder and groin as conditions turned dangerous for batting and he made the declaration at 382 for eight.

Now the nightmare of a Brisbane 'sticky dog' unfolded for the Indians, a combination of Bradman's smart tactics and Amarnath's failed gamble.

"The ball did all manner of unexpected tricks" was what *Wisden* 1949 reported and India were sent tumbling for a miserable 58.

It was the left-arm medium pacer Ernie Toshack who caused havoc, returning remarkable figures of 2.3 overs (eight-ball overs were in force in Australia back then) and five wickets for just two runs. In the second innings India could only manage 98 with Toshack this time grabbing 6 for 29 for lopsided figures of 11 for 31. With almost the entire fourth and full fifth day washed out, the drying pitch on the sixth and final day was at its most spiteful, giving the batsmen no chance.

Roland Perry in his book *The Don* wrote: "Amarnath may have had a twinge of regret not taking Bradman's advice about the wickets, although he was gambling on being able to take advantage of the weather if the law of averages were to be upheld."

The crushing defeat had a demoralizing effect on India but how unlucky they were was vividly described by Richardson.

"Had India won the toss the position would have been entirely reversed and Mankad's name would have been blazened forth instead of Toschack."

Richardson doubled down on his statement: "India need not despair over this defeat, as I repeat, had India won the toss the position and even the actual scores could have been reversed."

What if indeed!

Miserable Weather

The miserable weather followed the hapless Indians to Sydney. Never had so much play been lost in a Test on Australian soil in nearly 70 years.

This time having gotten lucky with the toss, Amarnath batted first. But that's where his luck ran out. Three full days out of six saw not a ball bowled due to the deluge.

Incessant rain for weeks before the December Test meant very little work had been possible on the playing square. The dark clouds were gathering overhead when India batted first and Amarnath was keeping his fingers crossed the rain would keep away for the duration of the innings. Sure enough it came down at lunch on the opening day with

India's stop-start batting eventually reaching 188—more than their two innings combined at Brisbane!

With the rest day following the second day and then a washout on the third and fourth, the players were left biding their time in the safety of the dressing rooms.

When play finally resumed on the fifth and penultimate day the home batsmen got a taste of their own medicine. With the rain-affected pitch playing tricks, they did not fare much better than the visitors did in the first Test.

The mighty side—Bradman's Invincibles, no less—collapsed for the third lowest score of his captaincy (24 Tests), a paltry 107 all out.

For Hazare, even more than the twin centuries in the fourth Test at Adelaide, his moment of glory came when he comprehensively bowled Bradman (13) with an off-cutter after a scratchy 40-minutes stay at the crease—the only innings in the series in which the Aussie captain did not reach three-figures save for the final Test when he retired hurt on 57.

As Hazare put it in his autobiography *A Long Innings*: "Like most of us, the giant proved fallible on a wet wicket."

With the conditions still bowler-friendly the Indian captain sent in tail-ender Amir Elahi to open the second innings with Mankad. But by close of the penultimate day seven wickets had crashed for just 61 runs. With rain always threatening, quick runs were the need of the hour and the batsmen lost wickets in a heap while going for boundaries.

Rain washed out the entire final day with India ahead by 142 runs and Hazare and Adhikari at the crease.

So **what if** the final day's play had not been washed out, would India have trapped Australia on another gluepot and stunned the Invincibles? Or would the mighty Aussies have gone 2-0 up in the series?

Hazare said India were unlucky to lose the final day's play while Richardson felt the opposite, that the rain had saved India from defeat.

Wrote Hazare: "It looked a safe score with the wicket favouring the bowlers and with the knowledge that the hosts would fare no better than us...We deserved a little favour from the weather gods after the injustice of the first Test...The Test was washed out and we lost the only chance of squaring the matters up." Hazare also pointed out that Bradman appeared happy with the rainfall on the last day and would periodically walk into the Indian dressing room to rub it in.

And rub it in he did in the third Test at Melbourne. Talk about rotten luck!

Australia won the toss again, batted first—of course—ran up 394 and then again trapped India on a wet pitch, gaining a lead of 103.

Richardson described the Test as "a triangular battle of tactics— Bradman vs Amarnath—with the weather intruding and eventually winning. Once more fortune favoured Australia and making an all time record of forcing India to bat again most of the time on rain-damaged wickets."

Amarnath declared nine down despite being behind on first innings as the pitch was beginning to play tricks after yet another soaking.

Bradman checkmated him by sending in the tail-enders first, protecting himself and the other specialist batsmen to eat up precious time, allowing the pitch to settle down.

The tactic worked. Though they lost four wickets for 32 runs, the tail-enders hung on till the sun came out shining brightly. Bradman and regular opener Arthur Morris then proceeded to both reel off unbeaten hundreds, the second of the Test for the Aussie captain.

The rain pelted down all night and on the rest day following the third day's play. Bradman declared on the overnight score of 255 for 4 on the fourth morning, once again trapping the hapless Indians on an unplayable pitch. How they must have cursed their luck, all out for 125 to lose by 233 runs.

Richardson was full of sympathy for the beleaguered tourists. "India has now played four and a half innings out of six innings so far on wickets which have given no chance of success…with equal conditions these games could easily become good struggles and had the luck been reversed even Bradman could not have saved Australia from at least two defeats."

This was a startling revelation but not much consolation for the deflated Indians who succumbed without a fight in the last two Tests of the series, losing both by an innings.

The Don Declares

The **what if** scenarios hugely favoured Australia and weighed heavily in their 4-0 victory. They also had a major bearing on Bradman's future in the game.

Right through the Australian summer there had been a sideshow running parallel to the Test series. Would Bradman mark his farewell to cricket with a fourth and final tour of England in the summer of 1948, following those of 1930, 1934 and 1938?

The nation was gripped with anxiety even as Bradman in characteristic fashion kept his cards close to his chest. But every Test in 1947-48 was seen by his vast legion of fans as his last at that particular venue: Brisbane, Sydney, Melbourne (where the third and fifth and final Tests were staged) and Adelaide, his adopted hometown.

Will he, won't he? There were two major issues which would decide one way or the other. One was his health and the other was his batting form.

The last 10 years had seen Bradman suffering one health issue or the other including during the war where he was struck with fibrositis. There had been grave doubts whether he would be fit for the 1946-47 home Ashes series against Walter Hammond's Englishmen, the first post-war series in Australia. There were also business commitments in his job as a stock broker.

Despite his health being far from perfect and doctors' advice to the contrary, Bradman took the call to participate in the Ashes series. In the tour game for South Australia that preceded the first Test he was like a pale shadow and scratched around for 76 and 1. One reporter wrote: "I have today seen the ghost of a great cricketer and ghosts seldom come back to life."

Despite all the misgivings, Bradman led Australia to a comprehensive innings victory in the opening Test at Brisbane, top scoring with 187. There was only one other century in the series but that was a huge 234 in the second Test. Australia won 3-0.

There were no further Test matches for Bradman till the arrival of the Indians in late 1947. Here too there was some suspense over his participation which he confirmed only in September. But still he would not be drawn into his availability for England in 1948.

With each Test, each innings over the course of the series there was mounting interest over his plans, tension mixed with excitement and anticipation. The press was hounding him for an answer at every opportunity, but he was giving nothing away, biding his time for the opportune moment to take the final call.

It was on the evening before the opening day of the fifth and final Test at Melbourne commencing on 6 February 1948 that he finally ended the suspense which by now had reached fever pitch—he would go to England on a grand farewell tour and series. And thus this Melbourne Test would be his final one at home.

Bradman won the toss and Australia won the Test (by an innings) but Bradman's desire to end his 20 years of playing Test cricket in his country with a farewell century did not quite work out. He tore a muscle and was forced to retire hurt on 57.

That tour of England was a personal triumph for Bradman, striding through the shires as if on a royal or papal tour. Massive crowds flocked to all 32 matches, the Invincibles remaining unbeaten and crushing England 4-0 in the Test series. Bradman had two centuries but the last innings of his storied career ended in bizarre fashion, bowled second ball for a duck. With just four runs needed to finish with an average of 100, he ended on 99.94 which became an iconic statistic.

Ironically if he had decided not to go to England and ended his career at Melbourne in February 1948 his career Test average would have stood at 102.98. But as the rueful Indians learned even before they landed in Australia in October 1947, not everything works according to plan.

But **what if** the fates (the toss) and Mother Nature (the vagaries of weather) had not conspired against Lala Amarnath and his hapless men? Would Bradman instead have taken the call to end his Test career at Melbourne rather than at the Oval six months later?

If Bradman had one chink in his formidable batting armour it was his discomfort batting on rain-affected pitches—'sticky wickets', 'sticky dogs', 'glue-pots', call it what you wish.

Being acutely aware of his own strengths and weaknesses was no doubt a major factor in his persuasive though futile efforts to get his Indian counterpart to agree to cover the pitches in the series. Amarnath was smart enough to know too that this was Bradman's Achilles Heel. In the one Test, the second at Sydney, when it was Australia's turn to be trapped the entire batting including of Bradman himself was exposed as fallible.

Even in the first Test at Brisbane with the rain affecting the pitch towards the end of Australia's first and lone innings, Bradman was troubled and hit around the body towards the end stages of his 185, hastening the declaration. And at Melbourne in the third Test he dodged a bullet in the second innings by pushing the tail-enders ahead of the specialist batsmen, thereby protecting himself till the conditions turned from challenging to placid.

In the end with a massive 715 runs for the series (average 178.75) inclusive of four centuries and a highest of 201 everything fell in place for the Don, making his call that much easier.

But Hazare and Richardson were both right after all. Under similar challenging batting conditions there was not much to choose between the Invincibles of Australia and the weakened rookies of India whose loss of four top players dampened their spirits from the start and had them on the back-foot right through the series.

Bradman made it to England in 1948 after all. And the rest is... what every cricket lover knows only too well.

CHAPTER FOUR

Durani and the Twists of Fate

Jasu Patel, the 'Prince' and others

It would be a tough task indeed to find two cricketers of the same era more dissimilar than off-spinner Jasu Patel and dynamic all-rounder Salim Durani, AKA 'The Prince of Indian Cricket' (the title of my 2024 biography of Durani)

And yet their careers are inextricably linked in strange and mysterious ways.

How so? The link goes back to Durani's first-class debut for Saurashtra against Gujarat in the Ranji Trophy match at Ahmedabad in November 1953. Even as Gujarat captain Patel took 6 for 57 from 26 overs on his home ground, the teenaged Salim held firm with 108 in his very first innings in the Ranji Trophy (and 41 in the second) on which he would leave an indelible stamp over the next 25 years for three different teams.

Patel was so impressed with the youngster he lured him away to Gujarat after Durani's one and only match for Saurashtra. Just two seasons later (1956-57) the peripatetic Durani had hopped across to Rajasthan. But there would be another uncanny link between the two

Patel's career was a strange one, just seven Tests between 1955 and 1960. In those seven Tests he took 29 wickets, with nearly half (14 to be precise) coming in a single amazing match against Australia in December 1959 in Kanpur and just two Tests later his career was over.

Richie Benaud's star-studded Aussies were the second to tour India after the Ian Johnson-led tourists of 1956-57. Patel had previously played two Tests against them for three wickets before being cast aside. In fact he had taken just ten wickets in his four Tests prior to Kanpur.

Now three years later in a surprise move the 35-year-old was back in the fold for the second Test at Kanpur after India had been crushed by an innings and 127 runs in the first in Delhi. Perhaps the most surprised of all was Patel himself who reluctantly travelled to Kanpur convinced he would be replaced by off spinner/batsman AG Kripal Singh in the playing XI. But on the morning of the match chairman of the selectors Lala Amarnath shocked one and all by picking Patel, his reasoning being some loose spots on a good length spot and the Aussies' purported weakness against off spin. The pitch was a newly laid one and would be used for the first time.

GS Ramchand had been appointed captain in place of DK Gaekwad following the disastrous 1959 tour of England where India were whitewashed 5-0 for the first time in their history. But the captain was none-too-keen on Patel's inclusion and had to be persuaded by Amarnath to pick him. Ramchand was no fan of Patel, the reason perhaps being the off spinner's dodgy bowling action—but more on that later.

On the face of it Kripal was the more logical choice. Patel himself admitted he was lacking in match practice. Kripal was a useful spinner and able batsman who had marked his debut against New Zealand in 1955 with a century. The Indian batting certainly needed bolstering after totals of 135 and 206 in the rout in the first Test.

So **what if** Kripal, the popular choice, had been selected instead of Patel? Amarnath had one of the shrewdest cricket brains in India and often went on a hunch. Sometimes his gambles paid off, sometimes they did not as happened in Australia in 1947-48 (see previous chapter). At Kanpur it certainly paid off, but was so close to not happening both before and during the Test.

Fortunately for India Ramchand won the toss and opted to bat. The visitors would be batting last on a pitch that was sure to deteriorate, assisting spinners Patel, Chandu Borde and Bapu Nadkarni.

The Kanpur Miracle

What happened when Australia batted was nothing short of sensational. The unheralded Patel whose selection was like a bolt from the blue ran through their batting with sensational figures of 35.5-16-69-9, the batting collapsing from 71 for one and 149 for two to 219 all out.

But things had looked bleak for India at lunch on the second day after being dismissed in their first innings for 152. The Aussie score was 128 for one at the break and though Patel had taken the wicket of Gavin Stevens for 28, opener Colin McDonald and Neil Harvey looked in total control. Patel was in despair and so was Amarnath as it looked like his gamble would misfire.

Patel had been pleading with his captain to bowl him from the other end where the pitch was already showing signs of wear-and-tear, but Ramchand refused to heed his pleas. So frustrated was Patel that at the lunch break he was changing out of his whites and into his street clothes, ready to storm out of the ground. This was recounted in his obituary published in the *Indian Express* on 12 December 1992 ('King of matting wicket' is dead by Anwar Almelkar).

Watching this dressing room drama, Amarnath was alarmed and used all his persuasive powers to convince Patel to stay on and also convince Ramchand to switch the off-spinner's end after the lunch break. It worked wonders as Patel ran through the strong Australian batting for the best figures by an Indian bowler in Test cricket till Anil Kumble's all-ten v Pakistan at New Delhi in 1999.

The result of the switch in ends was immediate and sensational. Off the very first ball after lunch, finally switched to the end that suited him, Patel bowled opener McDonald for 53 and the next eight wickets fell in a heap for the addition of only 91 runs. The only batsman to elude Patel was Norman O'Neill, bowled by Borde for 16.

Despite the tourists gaining a first innings lead of 67 runs, India's improved batting in the second innings with a total of 291 left their opponents with a target of 225 runs to go 2-0 up in the five-Test series.

They never stood a chance, crumbling to 105 to give India a sensational victory by 119 runs. Patel once again proved to be a handful and with figures of 5 for 55, spinning India to their first victory against Australia in their 10th encounter with Polly Umrigar chipping in with four wickets with his off spin.

The result brought immense joy and euphoria to the country which was craving success on the cricket field after the drubbing in England and before that, a 3-0 rout at the hands of West Indies at home in 1958-59.

But **what if** Patel had walked out of the Test in a huff, left the Indian team one short and effectively ended his own cricket career? And **what if** Amarnath even with his forceful personality had failed to convince captain Ramchand who was sullen and seething with Patel's inclusion in the Test in the first place?

India was already one-down in the series and would surely have lost this Test and faced a possible series whitewash that would have plunged Indian cricket into a deep crisis coming so soon after the debacle in England in the summer of 1959. Instead, the victory re-invigorated the game and led to more successes at home in the coming few years.

If one were to go by what Patel told reporter Almelkar a few years before his passing and which he wrote in the obit, the animosity Ramchand felt towards Patel ran deep. Patel told him that Ramchand had told his fielders to deliberately drop catches off his bowling. While such an accusation may sound startling today, such acts were not unknown in Indian cricket back then.

In the same obit, condoling Patel's death Amarnath recalled the dramatic events surrounding the Kanpur Test.

"I selected him at the last minute much against the wishes of my co-selectors as I was convinced he was the ideal bowler to exploit the spinning track at Kanpur. The entire press blasted me for the decision but with his superlative bowling, Jasu took India to victory and vindicated my choice and my honour."

For Benaud it was a bitter pill to swallow but he took it stoically In 28 Tests as captain he would never lose a series and be defeated in only four Tests as against 12 wins. This was his first setback in 11 Tests since being appointed captain in 1958-59 and must have been the most galling too and not just because of the result. For there was a lot of disquiet in the Aussie camp over Patel's bowling action. Nor were they happy with the Green Park pitch. But they kept a diplomatic silence at the time though over the years both Benaud and Ramchand would hint that Patel's action was not quite kosher, the latter somewhat more forcefully.

In the 1987 video *Great Moments in Indian Cricket* produced by Ashish Ray which can be seen on *youtube,* Ramchand gives grudging credit to Patel for his feat. "Jasu Patel had a slight defect in his wrist", says Ramchand, alluding to the story that he apparently broke his arm after falling from a tree when 10. Interesting such childhood accidents have been attributed to other bowlers with suspect actions.

Benaud with a wry smile in the same documentary says: "It (the bowling action) wasn't quite perfect." The Australians though also had two bowlers in their team with suspicious actions, fast bowlers Gordon Rorke and Ian Meckiff. This had created a storm of protest from the English camp during the 1958-59 Ashes series, Benaud's first as captain, won by a crushing 4-0 margin. So perhaps the silence at Patel's action was more than just diplomatic.

Umpire Strikes Back

There was a week between the end of the second Test at Kanpur and the third at Bombay with a three-day match between the tourists and Board President's XI squeezed in at Ahmedabad, Patel's hometown. Poor Patel would hardly have had any time to celebrate as he was captaining the side.

But to the surprise of one and all, he missed the third Test, ostensibly due to a bout of food poisoning. Even as the Australians piled up a massive 554 for six declared at Ahmedabad, the captain himself bowled just three overs and did not come out to bat in the first innings.

Durani scored 21 and 31 in the match at the same ground where six years earlier he has scored a century in his maiden first-class match.

Now a twist of fate saw him make his Test debut in the third Test at Brabourne Stadium in place of his ex-Gujarat teammate and state captain. And it was an umpire who apparently played a lead role in this drama.

Was it because of his illness, was it because the Indian team management wanted to protect him from the benign Brabourne strip which could allow the tourists to get on top of his bowling? Or was there something else behind Patel's exclusion?

Journalist Raju Bharatan would years later ask Ramchand why Patel did not play the third Test with the series locked 1-1. "Is it true, Ram, that you chose to hide Patel from the Aussie on that Brabourne Stadium featherbed?'

"Nonsense" came back Ramchand. "Jasu did not figure in that key third Test simply because he himself shied away from that game, apprehensive of being no-balled for 'throwing' by that very strict umpire ND Nagarvala." ('Another test of strength altogether' by Raju Bharathan, *The Hindu*, 7 March 1998)

So who was umpire Noshirwan 'Noss' Nagarvala? And how did he come to stand in that one and only Test in the series, incidentally the fifth and final of his career?

More pertinently for the purpose of this chapter, **what if** Nagarvala had not been chosen by the board to be one of the umpires for the Test, the other being Habib Chaudhury? Would Durani have had to wait for a few more years to make his Test debut or would he have missed the bus altogether if Patel had not been excluded? At 25 he was not young, at least not by Indian cricket standards where it is not uncommon for debutants to be in their teens or early 20's?

As it is, Durani batted only in the first innings for 18, bowled one over in the match and was promptly dropped for the fourth Test at Madras—as was umpire Nagarvala—with Patel making what Benaud sarcastically referred to in his autobiography as a "very quick recovery".

It would be nearly two years before Durani was back in the Indian team, this time against England at the same Brabourne stadium in November 1961.

Nagarvala indeed had history when it came to calling bowlers for chucking. He had been initially appointed for all three Tests when Australia visited India for the first time in 1956-57, but then was quietly removed from the umpires' panel once Patel was selected for the first and second Tests. The incident was narrated by Nagarvala in a book brought out on his life and times by his family (*Life Sketch*, Poona, 1989).

The fact that the same BCCI umpires' panel chose him to stand in the third Test in Mumbai that immediately followed Patel's sensational spell at Kanpur must mean a communication gap (or gaffe) existed between the panel and the selectors, leading to Patel's mysterious exit from the Mumbai playing XI even though he reported to the venue the day before the Test began.

Nagarvala—dubbed 'Principal' Nagarvala—was a legend in Poona's educational and sporting circles. Unlike most Indian umpires of the time, he had first-class playing credentials having represented the Parsees in the Quadrangular and Pentangular tournaments and Maharashtra in the Ranji Trophy.

His ninth wicket partnership of 245 runs with Vijay Hazare (316 not out; Nagarvala 98) for Maharashtra against Baroda in 1939-40 remained a Ranji Trophy record for 60 years. That season Maharashtra, captained by DB Deodhar, won the Ranji Trophy for the first time, beating United Provinces in the final in Poona with Nagarvala scoring 54 in the first innings.

Nagarvala also excelled in hockey and at club level, tennis, table tennis and golf. In a 1934 issue of *Illustrated Weekly of India* he was tipped for international honours in both cricket and hockey.

Twists of Fate

As for Durani, once he forced his way back into the Indian side in November 1961 he enjoyed a golden run in Test cricket for the next five years. In that comeback match against England in the first Test of the series at this favourite Brabourne Stadium he took three wickets and struck an aggressive 71.

But that run may not have happened at all if not for a dramatic and shocking **what if** incident later in the series that would have a profound effect on both Durani's career and that of two of his teammates.

The first and second Tests in the 1961-62 series at Bombay and Kanpur were drawn and the teams now shifted to Delhi for the third Test (which was also drawn).

The scene was the Imperial Hotel in the heart of the capital and the *dramatis persona* were master leg spinner Subhash Gupte, all-rounder Kripal Singh, plus an unnamed young woman. On the rest day of the match Kripal—single and in his 20s—called the hotel receptionist from Room number 7 and asked her to meet him for a drink.

The apparently harmless phone call blew up into a major scandal in which the unwitting victim was Gupte. Though Kripal's roommate, he was at the time of the call in another room playing cards with his teammates.

The receptionist complained to the manager, Gupte and Kripal were summoned before the BCCI's disciplinary committee and the pair were dropped from the next two Tests and the tour of West Indies that followed in 1962.

While Kripal made a brief Test comeback in 1964, the 32-year-old Gupte who was patently innocent was outraged and walked out of Test cricket and out of India altogether, moving to Trinidad where he had met his future wife on the 1953 tour of West Indies. They had married in 1957 and settled in Bombay. His sense of justice was inflamed and so after a glittering career in which he had bagged 149 wickets in 36 Tests and with at least five or six good years of Test cricket left in him, this gem of a bowler was never again seen in India colors.

At least for one player this sad and shabby event proved to be a boon. Durani's place in the side for the rest of the series was not assured as despite his good form in the first Test in Bombay, he had claimed only five wickets in the first three Tests with his left-arm spin.

What if that fateful phone call by Kripal had never been made or once it had been, if the receptionist had not taken offence? Both Kripal and Gupte would have remained in the side and most likely travelled to West Indies too.

Durani on the other hand may well have been dropped for the next two Tests at Calcutta and Madras and missed out on the Caribbean series that followed shortly, once again being consigned to the wilderness of domestic cricket, perhaps never to play another Test match.

Instead, he grabbed the golden opportunity with both hands, turned in match winning performances with both bat and ball, helping India win their first-ever Test series against England 2-0 in a brilliant display of attacking spin bowling.

At the Eden Gardens, where he would attain cult status with the spectators he had a match winning haul of eight wickets (5 for 47; 3 for 66) plus 43 in the first innings as India won by 187 runs. And then at Madras in the fifth and final Test he sealed the deal for India with ten wickets in the match, India winning by 128 runs and finally clinching their first series rubber against England after nearly 30 years of trying.

So from taking just five wickets in the first three Tests and being on the brink of dropping out of the team, Durani turned things around in dramatic fashion with 18 wickets in the last two, topping the bowling charts with 23 wickets.

It was only the third time India had won a Test series after beating newbies Pakistan in 1952-53 and New Zealand in 1955-56. But this was against England so extra special.

Durani was the hero but it so easily may not have happened at all and that set off the brilliant unbroken streak of 21 Tests (in which he would take 71 wickets) for the glamorous all-rounder, a huge hit with fans wherever he played. On the disastrous 1961-62 tour of West Indies where India were whitewashed 5-0, Durani was one of the few silver linings with a maiden (and lone) Test century and incisive bowling, a tour on which India sorely missed Gupte who had excelled on India's maiden visit in West Indies in 1952-53 with 27 wickets.

If Durani had been dealt the Ace of Spades at Delhi in December 1961, at Calcutta in December 1966 he got the Joker in the pack.

But Durani was not the only cricketer in that 1966 **what if** incident that would be affected, one which would have a profound effect on Indian cricket in the 1960s. And just as he (inadvertently) benefitted from the Delhi incident, it was Bishan Singh Bedi who was the beneficiary in Calcutta.

Garry Sobers brought his unofficial world champs West Indies to India in 1966-67 for three Test matches, winning 2-0. The first at Bombay saw them go one-up by six wickets with Durani (55) second top-scorer in the first innings after Borde's century. He appeared a certainty for the second Test at Calcutta and was included in the 16.

Unfortunately his wife fell seriously ill and had to be hospitalized in Bombay. As a result he could not make it to Calcutta till the evening before the Test. Manager Col. Hemu Adhikari came down heavily on the hapless Durani for arriving late and told him to go back to Bombay—he would not be playing at Calcutta.

The next morning shortly before the toss Ajit Wadekar, who had made his debut in Bombay, fell ill and was replaced by Hanumant Singh. If Durani had been allowed to stay on, he may well have made the XI after all under the circumstances.

His exclusion opened the door to left-arm spinner Bedi to make his Test debut. In the tour match staged between the Bombay and Calcutta Tests and while representing the Prime Minister's XI at New Delhi, Bedi bowled impressively in the tourists' first innings to bag six wickets. That included the master Sobers, hit wicket.

With the other left-arm spinner Bapu Nadkarni also dropped for Calcutta, the path was clear for the Punjab youngster. His late inclusion in the playing XI surprised Bedi more than anyone else. He was not in the original 16 and was asked to be present at the Eden Gardens as a 'nets' bowler. Expecting a quick departure, Bedi had his bags packed for Chandigarh to play in the Inter-Varsity tournament. But fate had other things in store for the 20-year-old from Amritsar.

Bedi, a future captain, would adorn the game for the next decade-and-a half into the early 1980s. His flight, guile and skill, entranced fans wherever he played while at the same time foxing the best of the world's batsmen. And after his playing days were over his would be the lone voice among ex-cricketers to voice protest at the many ills bedeviling Indian cricket—till that voice too went silent forever in October 2023.

Bedi became a favourite of his captain Tiger Pataudi while it was just the opposite with Durani. The Nawab and the 'Prince' could never see eye-eye-eye for reasons that have never been made entirely clear. It was only with Pataudi's ouster as captain to be replaced by Wadekar that Durani made a belated comeback to the Indian team five years later. Here too Durani benefitted from the misfortune of someone else, for no fault of his own of course, as we shall read in the next chapter.

But **what if** Durani had made it in time for the Calcutta Test? He would have certainly played, thus keeping Bedi waiting for his debut. By getting his lucky break, Bedi completed the famed spin quartet of EAS Prasanna, S. Venkataraghavan and BS Chandrasekhar that would weave their magic around the cricket world and entrance fans like no other bowling quartet had done before or since. And all because of the illness of a player's wife and the callous and hard-hearted attitude of the team manager.

CHAPTER FIVE

Against All Odds

Many Twists in Tiger's Tale

If Mohammad Mansur Ali Khan, the Nawab of Pataudi AKA 'Tiger' had not existed, the world would have had to invent him, preferably in the pages of a superhero comic book. But this one-eyed wonder did not fly through the air, leap over tall buildings and (repeatedly) save the world.

He did however arguably save Indian cricket from its moribund, parochial state. The fact that he was born into royalty, had dashing good looks, an aura and charm all of his own, married a leading movie star, was a brilliant stroke-player and a daring captain never hesitating to take a gamble in trying to win, all certainly gave him the aura of a hero in India, if not a superhero.

And that's before we even come to the accident that made him lose almost all the sight in his right eye. You see what I mean now about fiction? And his life had more ups and downs than the streets of San Francisco

Here is Tiger Pataudi's life in one admittedly long sentence: born into wealth; son of a famous and unique cricketer; father dies in his polo pony saddle on his son's 11th birthday; packed off to England for studies; breaks all school and college records; an accident then severely restricts his eye sight while on the cusp of batting greatness; a century in his maiden Test series; thrust into captaincy under tragic circumstances; reigns for a record period; marries Indian cinema's leading lady; sacked under controversial circumstances; back three years later also under unusual circumstances AND outlives most of his forefathers…well, that is some life!

It was perhaps pre-ordained that Tiger would play Test cricket just like his father Iftikhar Ali Khan, the Nawab of Pataudi (sr.) or just Pat. Pat's unique feat was to play for England and then captain India against England. A century on Test debut in the first Test of the infamous 1932-33 Bodyline series in Sydney held out great promise of a long and glittering career, especially after smashing all records in English cricket at school and college. But Pat's life and playing career were blighted by ill health and by the time he was chosen to lead India on their third tour of England in 1946 (see Chapter Two) he was frail and struggling. Five years later he was dead.

Like the senior Nawab, Tiger too was sent to England when young to study and play cricket too. His precocious talent can be guessed by the last line in his father's obituary in the 1953 edition of *Wisden Cricketers' Almanack*. "He left three daughters besides an eleven-year-old son, who has shown promise of developing into a good cricketer." Now that is some foresight!

That promise was fulfilled in 1957 when as a 16-year-old at school at Winchester he made his first-class debut for Sussex after breaking the school record for most runs in a season. The report in the *The Cricketer* 1958 winter annual accompanied with his photo receiving the 'Most Promising Young Cricketer of the Year' award mentions both his "outstanding batting" as well as his "very fine fielding", something which would mark him out throughout his Test career. It was not till the 1960 season however that he scored his maiden first-class century for Oxford University v Lancashire.

But by 1961 he had hit his straps and was enjoying one of the most amazing seasons by any cricketer in the long and storied history of Oxford University.

In the first match of the season against Gloucestershire he scored 48, then 79 not out against 1960 runners-up Lancashire. But he was just warming up.

On May 10—12, 1961 at Oxford's home ground, the Parks came the sensation of the season, a performance by the 20-year-old that scared the living daylights out of the reigning champions, the mighty Yorkshire.

The matches against Oxford and Cambridge were a chance for the county players to let down their guard and take it easy against the college kids. They were not part of the county championship and points did not count. But there was nothing easy for the battle-hardened Yorkshire as they were given the shock of their lives. Batting first, they declared at 286 for 4, no doubt confident they would easily roll over the collegians.

It was not to be and it was the young Nawab that lorded over the strongest bowling attack in the country, led by champion fast bowler Fred Trueman with Don Wilson and Ray Illingworth the Test spin bowlers in the side.

Tiger scored 106 out of 270 and as Yorkshire tumbled to 218 in their second innings, the target for the rookies was 235 in three-and-half hours.

If they came close it was all thanks again to the Tiger cub. Even as wickets tumbled around him, he took the attack to the Test bowlers including Brian Close as Oxford finished on 170 for 5, Tiger unbeaten on 103.

This is *Wisden* (1962 edition) on that dazzling performance: "Small and slim but possessing perfect timing…Pataudi reached his century in the first innings in just under two-and-a-half hours. (In the second innings) Pataudi was in magnificent fettle. He hit 12 fours in his 50 and finished with eighteen boundaries in his century, scored with strokes to all parts of the field. Towards the end of his two-hour-16 minute innings there was not a Yorkshire fielder within 30 yards of his bat…"

Wrote John Woodcock, the doyen of English cricket writers in the 2013 book of tributes to Tiger, *Pataudi: The Nawab of Cricket*: "Fred Trueman was still the best fast bowler in England. Tiger treated him with a disdain to which he was unaccustomed. The talk in The Parks, and not only there, was of little else." (Chapter titled 'The Common Touch')

The match ended in a draw but the eyes of the cricket world were opened to the dazzling talent in their midst. And in the very next match against Middlesex who also boasted a Test bowling lineup came his third century in a row which *The Cricketer* called magnificent.

In the roundup of Oxford's matches till then RH Maudsley in the issue dated May 27 wrote: "Pataudi deserves a paragraph to himself. He scored his third consecutive century at good pace and with insolent ease…He sees the ball very quickly, and seems able to despatch it at will to whatever part of the field he chooses. These are early days of course; whether he can maintain a proper balance between adventure and solidity remains to be seen. But he has already done some things which can only be done by people with a touch of genius"

Amazing praise indeed and there followed a string of half-centuries and to top it all, another century v MCC at Lord's. MCC had in their ranks two guest players, the West Indians Frank Worrell and Sonny Ramadhin, both excellent spin bowlers. "Pataudi drove, cut and pulled in dashing style, "reported the 1962 edition of *Wisden.*

There seemed no bowler that could stop the plundering prince as he cut a swathe across England's cricket grounds. But it was not a bowler, instead it was the cruel hand of fate that put a shuddering halt to that golden run.

The fateful day was July 1, 1961. The first day of Oxford's match against Sussex—Tiger's county—at Hove ended with Oxford 12 for 2 in reply to Sussex's 299. At the crease were Alan Duff on 3 and wicket-keeper Robin Waters who had been promoted as night-watchman ahead of captain Pataudi after the two openers were out cheaply. Waters was yet to open his account. Also in the Oxford lineup was Abbas Ali Baig who had made a sparkling century on Test debut for India at Old Trafford in 1959 when still an under-graduate.

Yet the next day the scorecard read: Waters (retired hurt) 0; Nawab of Pataudi: absent hurt. But why? And how?

It all began innocently enough. Tiger and four of his buddies, including Baig, went for dinner to a Chinese restaurant at Brighton, down the road from their Hove hotel barely 300 yards away. Bu while the other three decided to take a stroll and enjoy the pleasant sea breeze, Tiger wrote in his 1969 autobiography *Tiger's Tale*: "I was feeling much too lazy."

He thus made the fateful decision to squeeze himself into the front passenger seat of the tiny Morris Minor driven by Waters. The journey from the restaurant in Brighton to the hotel in Hove would have taken barely a minute but within seconds as they approached the statue of Queen Victoria at Hove's Grand Avenue, the accident happened.

"A big car pulled into the middle of the road and into our path. We hit it straight on" wrote Tiger. He said that though it was not a serious accident, he broke his shoulder and injured his hand. "I had no idea then that I had injured my eye as well, because I felt no pain."

Robin Marlar, who had been a team-mate in Sussex starting from Tiger's first year in 1957, gave a description of the accident site in the chapter titled 'Starting with Sussex' in *Pataudi: Nawab of Cricket*. "The junction is confusing; first on service road, then the busy multi-carriageway avenue along its front, very similar to Mumbai."

"The question that has haunted Indian cricket since July 1 1961 after the motor accident in Hove, was: what if they had been no accident?" is what I wrote in *The Cricketer* (September 2017) as part of their What If... series.

Looking back, I would now go back a step in time, just for a few seconds: **what if** Tiger had not been "feeling too lazy" and had taken the very short stroll from the restaurant along with Baig and the three others he had just dined with, allowing Waters to be the sole occupant of the car he was driving?

Even as he was being carried into the ambulance Tiger's first comment to Waters was he was now doubtful for the Varsity match. The annual Oxford v Cambridge fixture at Lord's was one of the most prestigious in the English cricket calendar back then, along with the match between Eton and Harrow schools and the Gentlemen (Amateurs) v Players (Professionals; long since disbanded), all three played at Lord's, the 'home of cricket.' The year before on debut in the college match he had struck a century, thus emulating his father.

His magnificent season had now come crashing down just as he was on the verge of breaking his father's record for most runs for Oxford in a season. It ended with 1,216 runs in 15 matches (24 innings) at 55.27, just short of Iftikhar's record of 1,307 runs set 30 years earlier. There were still three matches to go for Oxford with the Varsity match only a fortnight away in which Tiger would have been the first Indian to captain the college in the much-anticipated match.

Wisden 1962 lamented the accident and his absence: "Overshadowing all else in the events of Oxford University cricket in 1961 was the unfortunate accident at Hove which deprived the team of their highly talented captain, the Nawab of Pataudi, for all subsequent engagements including the match against Cambridge. His captaincy had been an inspiration to a side already well equipped in talent and experience and his fielding, as always, set a fine example... Above all, the Nawab, by his dazzling, if unorthodox batting, made the season memorable for all who saw him in action."

The incident brought back grim memories of an accident in England just two years earlier which took the life of the brilliant Jamaican all-rounder O'Neill 'Collie' Smith aged just 26 with Garry Sobers at the wheel.

Pataudi lost approximately 95 per cent of vision in the right eye. He lost the lens of the eye and a coat had developed over the iris. But at no time did the thought of giving up on cricket cross his mind, such was his steely resolve.

So who was Waters who was driving the car that fateful evening, escaping with some cuts and bruises? An Irishman, he was born in Calcutta and in the 1962-63 Ranji Trophy season represented Bengal in the quarterfinal and semifinal at Eden Gardens. His place behind the stumps in the Varsity match was taken by Charles Fry, grandson of the legendary CB Fry. Perhaps Waters' greatest claim to fame was being part of the Ireland team that stunned West Indies in 1969 by skittling them out for a shocking 25 in a famous match at Sion Mills in Ireland. He later became a well-know coach in Ireland and died in 2017 aged 80.

But the price he paid for the accident was, according to Robin Marlar in the Pataudi tribute book, much more than physical. "Robin Waters, a gifted young wicketkeeper, paid a devastating price, as I understood forty years later [i.e., 2001] when we met at a Sussex match in Dublin where he was boarding in a religious house. His deep scars were mental."

Waters' obit in *Wisden* 2018 claims Pataudi met him in Ireland during an Indian tour of England and told him he never held him responsible. However, there is no evidence that meeting actually happened as India on that 1967 tour did not have a match in Ireland where Waters lived.

Remarkably, Pataudi was back in the nets at Hove in late August. Sussex ex-pro and coach George Cox bowled to him hour after hour as Pataudi adjusted his stance and stroke-play, indeed his entire game, as he sought methods to overcome his handicap. As he put it in his typically understated manner in his autobiography: "...everyday life had proved a bit tricky at first." He also stated that it took him five years before "I could claim to be completely on terms with my handicap."

And those five years—approximately 1961 to 1966—were the prime of his youth when his batting may well have scaled legendary heights if not for the accident and injury.

A Test average of 34.91 may appear pedestrian in the modern era. But as he told Australian journalist Mike Coward in the 2013 book *Champions: The world's greatest cricketers speak*, the loss of the eye "caused me to perform 30 to 40 per cent below what I would have liked to have been and to accept that. That took a while to do and took a bit of doing."

Thirty to forty per cent? Do the math as the American's say.

In fact Pataudi's average was superior to some of his contemporaries like ML Jaisimha (30.68), Nari Contractor (31.58), Ajit Wadekar (31.07) and wicket-keeper Farokh Engineer (31.08) and among the specialist batsmen of that era only Polly Umrigar averaged in the 40s.

John Woodcock also made the awkward though pertinent point in the Pataudi tribute book: "He was fortunate, if that is the right word, that it was his right eye that took the main impact and not the left, the left being the master eye of the right-handed batsman, and also that he could see out of his right eye, albeit hazily. It was wonderful, even so, what he still managed to achieve, sometimes with much of his former splendor." (Chapter titled The Common Touch)

Asked in an interview in *Cricket Quarterly* magazine (Oct-Dec 1975) "to what extent, if at all, has the accident which injured your eye affected your cricket? A: "It has been a handicap, of course. For example against really fast bowling I would get yorked more often.

Since the accident it was comparatively difficult to quickly pick the length of the ball. I used to field close-in before which I had to give up."

In the matter of fielding Pataudi brought about a radical change iu Indian cricket's mindset, laying great emphasis on what was traditionally the weakest aspect. His electric cover fielding put him on part with his famous contemporary, the South African Colin Bland.

The story goes that he once invited the Indian team for a weekend stay at his Pataudi palace in Haryana. He put them through a fielding drill with a difference—each player had to wear a patch over their right eye. The results were both comical and poignant. And as always, Tiger had the last laugh, a hearty one at that.

Former England captain Tony Lewis who had known Tiger since their school cricket days in England contributed a chapter ('Laconic Heroism') in the tributes book in which he made a telling point.

"There is no doubt that before the car crash that so damaged his right eye, the Noob was about to be an exceptional talent, nor was I alone in making that adjudication. Trevor Bailey, for example, believed that he was going to match the batting skills of Garfield Sobers. With Tiger [before the injury] the ball disappeared softly off his bat as if from a muffled middle, or suddenly vanished with a crack of powerful contact."

After a couple of months in the nets fine tuning his new technique, Pataudi played his first first-class match for Delhi in the Ranji Trophy against Jammu and Kashmir from October 31, 1961, almost exactly four months since the accident.

He got a lucky break when chosen to lead the Board President's XI against the English tourists, led by his Sussex captain Ted Dexter. The match was staged in Hyderabad where Tiger would spend most of his Ranji Trophy career and with 70 in the first innings he forced his way into the team for the second Test at Kanpur. He missed that match due to an injury but made his debut in the next at New Delhi in December 1961.

But why "lucky"? Well, news travelled slowly and sometimes not at all, back then long before the 24x7 news cycle we are in now. Pataudi himself admitted in his book: "I doubt whether I would have been considered by the selectors had they known the extent of the damage to my right eye."

Indian selectors were notoriously conservative back then and with news filtering in from England, if they had got even a hint of the severity it is doubtful if they would have chosen him at all. Another amazing **what if** in an amazing life and career!

His mother and sister had flown to England to help him recuperate. It is quite likely they collectively decided to keep a tight lid on developments to prevent the severity of his injury from leaking out and reaching back home. If so, it was a wise move that paid rich dividends to Indian cricket.

It was just two Tests after his debut that he got his maiden Test century in the fifth and final Test at Madras in January 1962, astonishing the spectators with his audacious strokes, lofting the ball over the infield in a daring display of batting not seen in Indian cricket for decades. With a substantial contribution with the bat in the previous Test at Calcutta too, he played a leading role in India winning both the fourth and fifth Tests, thereby clinching the rubber 2-0, the first time India had beaten England in a Test series.

The Tiger had arrived in style and would not miss a single Test till December 1969 save for two in West Indies in 1962 and one in Adelaide in December 1967, all due to injuries.

Irving Rosenwater was famous for his obsession with facts and detail. In a perceptive analysis in *The Cricketer* ('Against the odds'; June 27, 1969) he traced the courageous saga of how many cricketers overcame physical handicaps.

He starts off writing about at least half a dozen cricketers who played first-class cricket with one eye, "excluding the Nawab of Pataudi, whose accident in Hove did not result in the loss of any eye, but destroyed the right lens and left impaired vision in that eye. His "dominant" eye—the left one for a right-hander—remained unharmed." Pataudi certainly did not lose the right eye but was left with just about five per cent vision in it.

The most prominent example of a one-eyed cricketer was the South African captain and pace bowler Eiulf Peter 'Buster' Nupen, (1902-1977), unique among Test cricketers as he was born in Norway. A devastating bowler on matting, he lost his left eye while playing as a child, a major handicap as he both batted and bowled right handed.

In more recent times three wicket-keepers suffered serious eye injuries standing up to spinners: Paul Downton (England), Mark Boucher (South Africa) and India's Syed Saba Karim.

Karim suffered his injury in the match against Bangladesh in the Asia Cup in Dhaka in May 2000 when a delivery from Anil Kumble cannoned off the flap of batsman Habibul Bashar's pad, rose awkwardly and hit him smack in the right eye. This was his 34th and last ODI and he was left with about five per cent vision in the eye.

He was back in Dhaka six months later for Bangladesh's inaugural Test match but struggled behind the stumps, obviously not fully recovered from the accident and retired from all cricket immediately after his lone Test.

Mike Brearley in his tribute in the Pataudi book in a chapter titled 'I Never Recovered' writes how Tiger visited Karim in hospital.

"Tiger helped the younger man to accept fate and move on; to make those adjustments that make life worth living. Saba asked him how long it took him to recover. 'Saba', he said. 'I never recovered'. But Tiger made a life, including of course, a major cricketing life, for himself, despite the accident."

Unlike his ancestors, Tiger lived to the age of 70. And for a full 50 of those years he lived with the handicap.

Among the twists and turns in an amazing life one of the most dramatic came in 1962 under tragic circumstances, thrusting him into the hot-seat of the Indian captaincy at the callow age of 21; a world record that lasted for four decades and still an Indian one.

India reached the Caribbean in February 1962 shortly after the conclusion of the home series victory against England which made captain Nari Contractor and his team the toast of the country. But they were without their leading bowler, leg spinner Subhash Gupte (see previous chapter) who had been such a striking success on India's maiden tour in 1953 when they lost just one of the five Tests.

Tiger missed both the first Test in Port of Spain and the second in Kingston through injury, routed by 10 wickets and an innings respectively.

It was a downcast team that headed to Bridgetown, Barbados to take on a side considered one of the strongest outside the Test arena. Barbados had a rich legacy both in batting and fast bowling with Garry Sobers and Wes Hall being the standouts in this side. Their captain was Frank Worrell, also captain of West Indies, but he was not taking part in this warm-up match prior to the third Test at the same venue, the Kensington Oval.

It was on the second day of the match that Contractor was struck a fearful blow by controversial fast bowler Charlie Griffith the details of which will appear in the next chapter.

What it meant was the Indian captain, who for a few days hovered between life and death with a fractured skull, never played for India again and suddenly the young Pataudi, with just three Tests behind him, found himself in the hot seat of the captaincy.

Pataudi was made vice-captain for the tour on the assumption that Contractor, who turned 28 on the tour, had five or six good years of cricket left in him during which his deputy could learn the ropes at international level before being eased into the job. He had already captained Oxford in England and Delhi in the Ranji Trophy.

But **what if** that sickening blow to Contractor never happened; indeed it almost did not as we shall see in the next chapter. Contractor was a sound left-handed batsman and despite the reverses in the West Indies series, there is little indication he would have been replaced as captain anytime soon.

The Tiger Pataudi era would have had to wait for a few more years. But now he was captain in a side where almost all others were senior to him. It was a daunting task for anyone, particularly under such shocking circumstances. For here was a rookie who was now face-to-face with one of the toughest tasks in world cricket.

The rest of the series must have gone like a blur for the traumatized tourists, crushed in all three remaining Tests to be whitewashed 5-0. Under the shocking circumstances it was difficult not to sympathise with them.

Pataudi soon eased into the job and registered some notable successes both at home and abroad. In fact in New Zealand in 1967-68 he guided India to their first win on foreign soil, culminating in their first series victory abroad too, 3-1 in the four Tests.

The editor of *The Cricketer* asked me to choose whom I considered the greatest Indian captain for a series of articles for their cover story dated November 2018 and headlined 'The Greatest National Captains. Who Was The Best?' from all the Test playing nations.

I had no hesitation in plumping for Pataudi with other writers choosing the following: Mark Taylor (Australia); Mike Brearley (England); Brendon McCullum (New Zealand); Imran Khan (Pakistan);

Graeme Smith (South Africa); Arjuna Ranatunga (Sri Lanka) and Clive Lloyd (West Indies).

Regionalism had always been the bane of Indian cricket leading to petty jealousies and even alleged sabotage with deliberately dropped catches. But Tiger was above all that and that was his greatest and most lasting contribution.

Tiger, in the words of his close friend and greatest admirer, Bishan Singh Bedi "was the first Indian captain who brought the culture of 'Indianess' to the dressing room. 'Listen fellas, we are not playing for Delhi, Chennai, Mumbai, Bengal or Maharashtra. We are playing for India. Think India for goodness sake…" (In the Pataudi tribute book chapter titled 'Let Me See If the Umpires Are Awake!')

It was in cultivating the legendary spin quartet of Bedi, BS Chandrasekhar, EAS Prasanna and S. Venkataraghavan and in placing great emphasis on fielding, both ground and catching, that Tiger changed the face of Indian cricket, leading to the first wins for India in West Indies and England in 1971 led by his successor Ajit Wadekar who inherited a readymade team.

The twin series at home in 1969-70 however proved to be disappointing both for Pataudi and the team. They were lucky to escape with a 1-1 draw in the 3-Test series against New Zealand and then lost 3-1 to Australia. The 5-Test series could so easily have ended 2-2 but for some missed opportunities. And now the captain's future was thrust into doubt after being at the helm for 36 of his 39 Tests till date.

The 'palace coup' which dethroned the Nawab in January 1971 was plotted by Chairman of the Selectors Vijay Merchant. And the manner in which it was pulled off is typical of Indian cricket's murky ways.

At the centre of the storm was East Zone selector K. Dutta Ray, a highly polarizing figure from Calcutta's sporting world of football and cricket. However, he was controversially absent from the meeting in

Bombay on January 8 which stunned Indian cricket by sacking Pataudi and choosing Bombay's Ajit Wadekar in his place for the series in West Indies.

A known Pataudi backer, Dutta Ray's absence saw the four other selectors deadlocked 2-2 and it was left to Merchant as the chairman to use his casting vote to cast Tiger into the wilderness.

Dutta Ray antagonized his fellow selectors by lobbying for Keki Tarapore as manager for the tour though Col. Hemu Adhikari was the consensus candidate. Enraged, they saw to it that he was banished from the selection committee meeting.

But **what if** he had been present? It is almost certain his vote would have gone to Pataudi, thus making it 3-2 in his favour. That India stunned the cricket world by winning both in West Indies and England in 1971 papered over the cracks of the tawdry episode with the Wadekar reign continuing till 1974.

In those three golden years India under the new skipper pulled off the unprecedented feat of winning three series in a row, including England 2-1 at home in 1972-73 where Pataudi made a successful comeback purely as a batsman in the last three Tests.

The 1974 tour of England though was a disaster both on the field (3-0 whitewash) and off it and Wadekar's goose was cooked.

And so in a delicious twist of irony, Pataudi was back to replace the man who had ousted him three years earlier and this time Merchant was not on the scene either, his stint over.

Pataudi made two points clear to the selectors who urgently called on him to fill the breach—he had to be appointed for the full series at home against West Indies in 1974-75 and not initially just the first two Tests as they had planned. And that this would be his final bow in Test cricket, come what may.

India narrowly lost the series 3-2 though Pataudi was absent through injury for the defeat in the second Test at New Delhi,

Venkataraghavan leading in his absence. So his own personal record was 2-2 in his final series as remarkably he led the side in all but six of his 46 Tests.

The curtain finally fell on the royal Tiger's career full of dizzying ups and downs. It was though a magnificent reign which left its indelible mark on Indian cricket.

As I wrote in *The Cricketer* while justifying my choice: "The Nawab of Pataudi was the first captain to bring a sense of national pride and unity to the Indian dressing room. Others merely followed in those giant footsteps."

CHAPTER SIX

Gone with the Windies Part I

Tales from the Caribbean

India's second tour of West Indies in 1962 was jinxed from the start; it would turn out to be perhaps the most disastrous of any cricket tour in history and not just because of the 5-0 whitewash.

In a previous chapter we have seen how India's leading bowler, the leg spinning magician Subhash Gupte had his career sabotaged by an injudicious phone call by a room-mate and the scandalous manner in which he was hung out to dry.

That meant the hero of the previous tour (1953) was jettisoned. On that tour where India were up against the mighty batting triumvirate known as the Three W's (Clyde Walcott, Everton Weekes and Frank Worrell) Gupte took 50 wickets in all including 27 in the Tests on plumb batting tracks, thwarting the mighty home batting machine to the extent that India lost just one of the five Tests. This just months after being routed in the previous series in England.

Chapter Five narrates how vice-captain Tiger Pataudi was thrust into the captaincy under tragic circumstances. But the exact circumstances behind the shocking incident that almost cost captain Nari Contractor his life—and ended his Test career—are worth examining in more detail.

Contractor told me an in an interview that he always had a superstition about taking first strike as opener but decided to do so this time as there was time for just one over before lunch "and I did not want to expose my young partner Dilip Sardesai" who was on his first tour ('40 years after Bridgetown', *bbc.com*, March 17, 2002). This after Barbados, overnight 319 for 6 were all out for 394 on the second morning of the four-day match.

Charlie Griffith opened the bowling and after Contractor had been warned the night before at a party by West Indies' captain Frank Worrell that Griffith was a dangerous bowler, his first over proved pretty innocuous. There was just time for that one over and both Contractor and Sardesai laughed off the threat from Griffith.

But Sardesai was out in the first over after the break to Wes Hall and this brought in all-rounder Rusi Surti, also on his first tour. Now Griffith was back for his second over and Contractor sensed danger as the first three balls whizzed past his nose at express pace. Suddenly he was alive to the threat.

Then came a **what if** moment—Barbados captain Conrad Hunte at short leg muffed a chance from the fourth delivery, taking the ball on the half-volley when he could have gone for the catch.

"Looking back, I wish he had taken the catch" Contractor told me ruefully in the interview that marked the 40th anniversary of the incident.

Surti at the other end shouted at him, "Skipper, he is chucking." This upset his concentration. "I walked up to Surti and said 'you don't shout across the wicket like that. If you think he is chucking, then tell the umpire." (Interview to Clayton Murzello, 'On the Spot with Nari Contractor'; *Back Spin* magazine; Autumn 2014). Contractor described Surti as "a hot-headed person." They were two of the four Parsis on tour, the others being former captain Polly Umrigar and wicket-keeper/batsman Farokh Engineer.

Then came the fifth ball which fractured the batsman's skull and led to a series of life-saving operations in Bridgetown and back home in India as the cricket world reacted in shock and horror.

As Griffith raced in to deliver the near-fatal ball someone in the pavilion opened a window. Contractor said that created a "black square" for him, a blind spot. In the instant before the ball left Griffith's hand the thought struck him that he should move away from the crease. Without a sightscreen at the pavilion end where Griffith was bowling and with his concentration already shaken by Surti's outburst, he hesitated for that fraction of a second which almost proved fatal as the ball thudded into his head. That led to the drama that unfolded at the hospital as he hovered between life and death for days.

But **what if** the window had not been opened at that the crucial moment and **what if** Contractor had retreated from the crease, forcing the umpire to call 'dead ball?' Well, that would not only have prevented the horrific injury that ended his Test career, it would also have changed the course of Indian cricket history—for better or for worse, one will never know (see Chapter Five).

Remarkably, Contractor, known for his courage and steely resolve, returned to first-class cricket just 14 months after his life had been plunged into peril. He continued playing domestic cricket till 1970-71 with some success but the BCCI, without saying in so many words felt it would be too risky to choose him again in the national side, a lingering regret for Contractor now into his 90s.

Pataudi was uncharacteristically harsh of Griffith in the opening chapter of his autobiography ('The Barbados drama'), the rest of the book being low-key and uncontroversial. He does however get the first line of the book wrong when he writes 'March 16, 1962, will be remembered as a black day in the annals of Indian cricket...". In fact the incident occurred on March 17, the second day of the match.

In it he is unequivocal in his condemnation of Griffith's bowling action, making no bones about the fact he considered the West Indian an out- and-out chucker. He was backed by a number of other respected voices in international cricket including England's Ken Barrington and Australia's Richie Benaud who went public with their views in the 1960s.

Worrell was enraged at Griffith's act and severely castigated Hall in the evening of the incident for bowling bouncers in tandem with Griffith. He also stated he would never choose Griffith in his West Indies team but went back on his promise for the 1963 tour of England where Griffith was in devastating form and played a major role in their 3-1 victory with 32 wickets in the five Tests. These stories were narrated by KN Prabhu in his article in *Sportsweek's World of Cricket* (October-December 1978).

But by the time Griffith came to India in 1966-67 with Garry Sobers' side his bowling was tame and he held no terrors for the home batsmen, taking only nine wickets in the three Tests.

Pataudi in his autobiography commented on this: "As for Charlie Griffith, anyone seeing him bowl for the first time must have found it difficult to imagine how he had once struck terror into the hearts of some of the world's best batsmen. His deliveries were a model of correctness, but almost entirely innocuous." Contractor too in his interview in *Back Spin* noted the change in Griffith's bowling.

So what was behind the drastic transformation? The twist in the tale came in 1989 in an article by Pataudi in *Sportsworld* magazine of which he was editor ('Caribbean Campaign', March 16-21, 1989).

"In 1962 and 1963 Charlie was lethal. By the time he came to India in 1966, he had become a gentle giant who was too scared to let go a bouncer however innocuous, because we had informed him (via an intermediary) that if he injured an Indian batsman his own life would be in jeopardy."

Startling indeed and one can only speculate as to who the "intermediary" was!

But there is more. Pataudi in the same article wrote: "He [Griffith] was in fact a coward." The context to this accusation was the riot in the second Test of the series in Calcutta over the new year. Terrified by the shocking scenes unfolding across Eden Gardens, Griffith began jogging his way back to the team hotel, the Great Eastern, across the Maidan. "On the way a couple of boys approached him to get his autograph and Charlie, convinced that they were after his blood, accelerated from a jog to a sprint and collapsed in the foyer of the hotel," Pataudi wrote.

Victory at Last

The change in captaincy from Tiger Pataudi to the unheralded Ajit Wadekar was a coup pulled off by Chairman of Selectors Vijay Merchant. Whatever may have been Merchant's reasons behind the sacking of Tiger which in January 1971 rocked Indian cricket like an earthquake, he was eventually vindicated.

For under Wadekar's captaincy India won a Test—and series—against West Indies on their soil for the first time (India in fact had never won a single Test against them at home or outside since the first series in India in 1948-49) and later that summer repeated the feat in England to send shockwaves through the cricket world and herald India's emergence as a new cricket power.

The absence of East Zone selector M. Dutta Ray (see previous chapter) at the all-important meeting in Bombay and the subsequent sacking of Pataudi also opened the doors for brilliant all-rounder Salim Durani who had been on the sidelines since the first Test against West Indies in December 1966.

For various reasons, some explained, some hazy both Dutta Ray and Pataudi appeared to have had a personal axe to grind against Durani which meant he was lost to Indian cricket for four long years. Now Dutta Ray—who was also absent from the team selection meeting in Madras on January 13—and Pataudi were both out of the picture, opening the door for Durani and this turn of events would prove crucial come the second Test at Port of Spain.

Understandably he was a relieved man when he heard the news, having despaired of ever getting back into the national side. This is how Ashwin Raman described his reaction: "No, Salim Durani did not jump with joy, when he heard he was back in the Indian team, for the West Indies after four years in the wilderness. He just slumped on the nearby sofa and stared into empty void, exhausted by the tension that had accumulated, weeks before the selection." ('They are back from the wilderness', *The Times of India*, January 14, 1971):

Another crucial factor at the selection committee meeting was new skipper Ajit Wadekar putting his foot down for the inclusion of middle-order batsman Dilip Sardesai whose last Test had been the first against Australia at Bombay in November 1969.

Merchant was not keen on his selection but Wadekar's contention was this being his maiden series as captain he needed all experience he could get and Sardesai was one of four in the tour party with previous experience of the Caribbean, the others being ML Jaisimha, Durani and EAS Prasanna. So with Wadekar standing his ground against the chairman, Sardesai was chosen as the 16th and final member of the touring party. Merchant was not too pleased at being challenged, that too by a newly appointed captain and wanted Chandu Borde in the side.

There was more drama before the team even landed at their destination. At 21-years-old Bombay opening batsman Sunil Gavaskar was the youngest in the squad and one of five who were yet to play a Test match.

Three days before the team departed for Kingston, Jamaica via London and New York he began to feel a throbbing pain in the middle finger of his right hand. The doctor diagnosed it was a whitlow and had him exempted from net practice at CCI, Bombay. But after a night's say in London and on the flight to New York the pain became unbearable. On arrival manager KK Tarapore rushed Gavaskar to a hospital where the surgeon recommended immediate surgery and said if he had not got it done even 24 hours later the finger would have had to be amputated as gangrene could have set in. That meant the youngster had to sit out the early part of the tour and missed the opening Test at Kingston, Jamaica which opened up an opening slot for another newcomer, K. Jayantilal.

GR Vishwanath, with a century on Test debut v Australia in the previous season, was also on his first tour. He was carrying a knee injury and missed nearly half the Test series as a result. But it was only a few hours before the start of the opening match of the tour against Jamaica at Kingston that he informed Wadekar that he was not fit to play. This let in Sardesai who had not been included in the playing XI for the match—and he grabbed the opportunity with both hands scoring 97 before being run out. This ensured his selection for the first Test at the same venue.

So India went into the opening Test match at Sabina Park without two of her young batsmen, Gavaskar and Vishwanath. And here fate was to take more twists and turns starting with the weather. The entire first day's play was washed out, reducing the Test to a four-day affair.

Put into bat, India collapsed to 75 for 5 and it appeared the ghosts of the 1962 tour were back to haunt the team.

That's when Bombay team-mates, the left-handed all-rounder Eknath Solkar in his first overseas Test and the veteran Sardesai came together in a magnificent partnership which not only turned the tide of the Test but of the series as well, in fact of the entire history of Indian cricket. They took the score to 183 without further loss at the end of the second day and carried on the next day to take the total to 212 before Solkar was out for 61.

The sixth wicket partnership was worth 137 runs and with Sardesai moving onto the first double century by an Indian abroad and first v. West Indies, India reached 387, a total that would have seemed like a mirage in the first part of the previous day. To rub salt into the bowlers' wounds, Sardesai also added a record 122 runs for the ninth wicket with Prasanna.

Sardesai's innings was just the start of a fantastic series, ending with 642 runs at 80.25 including two centuries and a double.

At the end of the tour none other than Merchant, the same man who tried to keep him out of the touring party, dubbed him India's 'Renaissance Man'. But what if the chairman of selectors had had his way as he was used to and Wadekar's insistence on Sardesai's inclusion had been in vain? And **what if** Vishwanath had been fit, was included in the tour opener, scored well and kept Sardesai out of at least the Kingston Test if not the rest of the series?

In an interview looking back on the 1971 tour, Gavaskar in an interview with Sanjjeev K. Samyal in *Hindustan Times* ('It was tough to live up to the expectations that were raised'; March 14, 2024) said it was Sardesai who was the main difference between the two teams. "But for his 212 in the first Test when we were 75/5 and then his 150 in the fourth Test [at Bridgetown, Barbados] when we were looking at a follow on; we would not have won the series."

Make no mistake, this innings by Sardesai and this Tests match marked an epochal moment for Indian cricket, even though it eventually ended in a team draw. But why so?

The Follow-on

The lead was 170 runs and with no play on the first day and the match now of four days duration, the follow-on deficit as per the laws had been reduced from 200 to 150 runs. This only applied to five-day Tests where there was no play possible on the first day.

It was the 24th Test between the two teams since 1948-49 and never before with a record of 12 wins and no defeats had West Indies been forced to follow-on. In fact it was the first time in the history of Test cricket that this law had been applied.

The psychological effect it had on Sobers and his men was immense. Even though they saw out a draw on the final day there were moments during the follow-on when an innings defeat looked distinctly possible. Even though the side was going through a barren spell since 1968, nothing could have prepared the home supporters for such a shock.

It had the opposite effect on the cock-a-hoop Indians. Wadekar admitted in his 1973 autobiography *My Cricketing Years* that he had told his side before the Test that they should settle for a draw "on the fast Sabina wicket and wait for our chance to play on the spinning tracks elsewhere". This was particularly the case at the Queen's Park Oval, Port of Spain, Trinidad where the second and fifth Tests were being staged and which traditionally aided the spinners.

Now suddenly the tourists, who had been dismissed as a mere club side by some local pundits before the first Test, were all fired up and they carried that momentum and self-confidence with them throughout the rest of the series.

But there is an intriguing tale behind the follow-on which needs narrating here. According to vice-captain S. Venkataraghavan it was he who alerted the skipper about the new target.

Wrote Aditya Bhushan in his 2019 book (with Sachin Bajaj) *Fortune Turners: The Quartet that spun India to victory:* "Interestingly, it was Venkat who had brought up this law to Wadekar's notice. And during my meeting with Venkat, when I told him about this story, his immediate response was: *"Not a story, it's a fact. In those days, as a player I used to take so much interest in reading the rules. I used to know the laws of the game from top to bottom."* Venkat it should be noted here remains the only Indian Test cricketer to become an international umpire.

He also told S. Giridhar and VJ Raghunath in their 2014 book *Mid-Wicket Tales: From Trumper to Tendulkar:* "When India took a lead of 170 runs it was I who informed Wadekar our skipper about the rules that stated when a Test match was reduced to four days [actually only when there is no play on the first day], the follow on was enforceable with a lead of over 150 and did not have to be 200. Wadekar mumbled something about "do sau", which is 200 in Hindi but I said, "Ajit, believe me I'm right. Sure enough, umpire Sang Hue agreed..."

The twist in the tale comes from Tony Cozier, the late doyen of West Indian cricket writers, in his report in *The Cricketer* ('The Indians Shake West Indies', April 1971).

"The West Indian debacle which was to follow was the result of several factors. Not the least of these was the mistaken impression that the follow-on deficit was 200. Only when the last pair was at the wicket was it officially confirmed to Sobers and his men that, since the first day had been completely lost, the match was now of four days and subsequently the follow-on deficit had been reduced to 150."

What Cozier leaves unsaid is who it was who "officially" informed Sobers of the new deficit. It could not have been the umpires since the match was ongoing and besides, Sobers was not at the crease. And there was no Match Referee back then either. Or perhaps it was the umpires after all who may have sent a message to Sobers in the dressing room through an official or a player?

The intriguing question here is if Sobers was officially informed, why was not Wadekar? For Venkat has further stated that Wadekar was skeptical and had to be persuaded about the quirk in the law before he approached Sobers and told him his team would have to follow-on.

So **what if** the vice-captain had not tipped off his captain and persuaded him to ask West Indies to bat again, despite Wadekar not being initially convinced? Well, if India had batted the second time, the Test would have petered out into a draw, and more vitally, the humiliation faced by the hosts would have been avoided, something they could never quite get over in the remaining four Tests in the series which India sensationally won 1-0.

Wrote Cozier in his 1978 book *The West Indies: Fifty Years of Test Cricket*: "India's confidence after their first innings of 387 was restored. When the West Indies were forced to follow on in reply it could hardly have been higher. It was a commodity that was vital during the tour."

Enter, Sunil Gavaskar

The fact that India did not bat a second time at Kingston meant that debutant Jayantilal opening with Syed Abid Ali, played his lone innings, caught by Sobers off opening bowler Grayson Shillingford for 5. And what a catch it was! As Jayantilal tried to take his bat away from the outgoing delivery, it took the edge and raced to Sobers at second slip. He first moved to his left, but then changed direction to his right with lightning speed to grasp the edge with both hands.

In his 1976 autobiography *Sunny Days* Gavaskar wrote: "Jayantilal withdrew his bat at the last moment, but the ball came back sharply, got an edge and travelled like lightning between second and third slip. There was a flash of movement and Sobers came up laughing with the ball clutched to his chest. 'What a catch' I told somebody."

That dismissal was significant for two reasons: it would end up being the first and only Test (and innings) of the Hyderabadi's career though he also travelled with the team for their three-Test tour of England that summer. And Sobers' catch was a rare highlight in the field for the masterly all-rounder and brilliant fielder who time and again in the series muffed catches in the slips.

And who would be the recipient of Sobers' unintentional generosity? None other than Gavaskar who re-wrote the history and record books with 774 runs in four Tests including three centuries and one double. Even after more than half a century, they remain both a world record for a debutant and a series record for India.

In the words of the great man himself in the 2024 book *Sunny G: 75 Years, 50 Tributes* (Chapter titled 'How a dropped catch started the journey'): "In the 1971 Test series against India in the West Indies there was a tale of two chances at slip.

In the first Test at Jamaica I caught Kenia Jayantilal off the bowling off our new-ball bowler Grayson Shillingford in the first innings. He had made six [actually five] and India did not bat again in the drawn match.

In the second Test at Trinidad, there was a chance offered by the opener who had replaced Jayantilal. This time, I dropped it. Sunil Gavaskar went on to make the most of that early reprieve and anchored India to their first-ever Test win in the Caribbean. He scored 65 and 67 not out and won it for India on debut.

For poor Jayantilal that turned out to be his only Test. Sunil became one of the legends of the game. It was a simple chance that somehow popped out of my hands. Looking back, the catch taken and the chance missed changed the lives of two young players in contrasting ways."

Over to *Sunny Days*: "The next morning [second day of the second Test at Port of Spain] I was relieved to see Sobers grass a low fast edge off [Vanburn] Holder as I tried to drive him off the back foot. Sobers tumbled in the attempt but spilled the ball. This was a lucky break and I went on with greater confidence and got my 50 after lunch."

But this was not a one-off aberration! It happened twice in the drawn third Test at Georgetown, Guyana again at slip as Gavaskar moved to his maiden century in the first innings. The first time the bowler to suffer was Shillingford. Then when he was on 94 Sobers grassed a chance off Noreiga, this time while fielding at short square-leg. So that was three dropped catches in three innings by a man who rarely dropped a single one all series.

Gavaskar also crossed 700 runs in six Tests v West Indies at home in 1978-79 with 732. The only other Indian to emulate him was Yashasvi Jaiswal against England in the home series in 2023-24. The 22-year-old left hander plundered 712 runs in the five-Test series including two double hundreds. The March 2024 interview with Gavaskar in *Hindustan Times* was shortly after Jaiswal's feat and was also a focus of the interview. In it Gavaskar too mentioned the dropped catches.

Q: When a player gets 700-plus runs in a series, for you what does it say about a player?

A: "When a player gets runs in a series then he is very good or very lucky. In my case it was the latter as no less a cricketer than Garry Sobers gave me lives in my first Test half-century and then in my first century."

What makes Gavaskar's feat exceptional however is that it was not only his debut series, it was outside India. Further, he missed the first of the five Tests and finished with the astounding average of 154.80. So **what if** he had played all five, how many more runs would he have scored? The mind boggles at the thought! Keep in mind the world record set by Don Bradman (who else?) in England in 1930 (974 runs in five Tests) still stands unmatched after nearly a century.

Durani's magic

Durani had not done much on his second tour of West Indies till then. But it was the genius in him that bowled two unplayable deliveries in the second Test that accounted for both skipper Sobers and danger man Clive Lloyd in quick succession to turn the tide in India's favour.

West Indies' first innings total of 214 was their lowest against India to date. India replied with 352 with another century by 'renaissance man' Sardesai and fifties by Gavaskar and Solkar. For the second Test in a row India had a substantial lead, this time of 138 runs. By the end of the third day the hosts had wiped out the deficit and were comfortably placed at 150 for one.

Prasanna had hurt his finger in attempting a caught-and-bowled off Roy Fredericks and was out of action on the fourth day. This opened the way for Durani to get an extended spell even though he had not bowled a single over in the first innings with Bedi, Prasanna and Venkat taking eight of the ten wickets.

It was an incident in skipper Wadekar's hotel room the night before that proved crucial. Durani confidently told Jaisimha he would get both the batsmen out the next morning if given the ball. Jaisimha was the senior-most member of the squad as was part of the team brain's trust. Wadekar valued his judgment and readily sought out his advice. Jaisimha had been dropped for the second Test but had Wadekar's ear and when he conveyed Durani's bold statement in the presence of Vishwanath and Prasanna, Wadekar decided it would be worth the gamble.

It certainly paid dividends. Sobers had an awesome record against India and had never been out without scoring in this his fifteenth Test and twenty-fourth innings against them. But now it happened.

It was the 60th over of the innings and the fourth of the fourth morning. Left-hander v left-hander. For five balls Durani bowling round the wicket had the maestro on a tight leash. Sobers hated being tied down and was getting restless. Durani pitched the final ball of the over on a length that pinned the batsmen to the crease. Sobers played no stroke as the ball broke to clip the off bail. Sobers bowled Durani 0! The batsmen could not believe his eyes, muttering in dismay as he trudged back; the bowler was so excited he had to be calmed down by his teammates.

That made it 152 for three and 17 runs later Durani had Lloyd smartly caught by Wadekar at short mid-wicket for 15. Now from 150 for one the slide saw West Indies collapse for 261. The winning target of 124 was easily reached by India with seven wickets in hand and against all odds the 'club side' were one-up with three to play.

But **what if** Prasanna, India's best bowler in the first innings with 4 for 54 had been fit to bowl on the fourth and what turned out to be the final day? And **what if** Wadekar had not set aside his ego while taking advice from Jaisimha? It is quite likely Durani would not have got a bowl at all and that magical spell which is written in letters of gold in the history of Indian cricket would never have occurred. For that matter, Durani might not have been selected at all but the strange turn of events back in Bombay in January.

Gavaskar finished the series in a blaze of glory. He became the first Indian and only the second at the time (after Australia's Doug Walters) to score a century and double century in the same Test. The fifth and final Test at Port of Spain was drawn and India against all odds were victors in Wadekar's maiden series as captain, a feat he would repeat later that summer in England to make 1971 one of the most memorable years in the history of Indian cricket.

As for Gavaskar, it should be remembered that if not for manager Tarapore's quick thinking in New York, Gavaskar could have lost that infected finger. The repercussions of this particular **what if** are too horrible to consider!

But spare a thought for poor Jayantilal. Despite finishing third in the tour averages to Gavaskar and Sardesai with 56 including a century v Guyana and four 50s, he was edged out of the opening slot not by Gavaskar but by Ashok Mankad who opened in the second, third and fourth Tests before being dropped for the fifth and final with Abid Ali moving up as Gavaskar's opening partner.

And **what if** Sobers had taken that catch in Gavaskar's maiden Test innings and the next two in the next Test on the way to his maiden century? Well, that surely is part and parcel of the game of glorious uncertainties!

CHAPTER SEVEN

A Tale of Two (West) Indians

Richards' Riches; Rowe's Woes

The great Vivian Richards a "nervous wreck?" Really? The batsman whose swagger was enough to give the fiercest of bowlers the chills?

Yes, it happened and at the nascent stage of his career as he walked nervously to the crease in the second Test in New Delhi after failing in both innings in the first in Bangalore. This was the 1974-75 series in India where Clive Lloyd was in his first as captain of West Indies and Tiger in his last as captain of India.

It was the first and probably the last time the great man felt this way. But he had good reason to. In the first Test which West Indies won by 267 runs, Richards on debut was foxed by that brilliant leg spinner and Indian cricket's greatest match winning bowler BS Chandrasekhar, out to him in both innings for 4 and 3.

"Back in the dressing room [in Bangalore] I slumped on the bench and came to a definite conclusion: Test cricket was too hard for me. I wasn't up to it. I'd been found out at that level. My own fears that I was nothing like ready for international cricket were being confirmed" (From the 1979 book *Viv Richards* with David Foot)

Richards so low on confidence is hard to believe today. But it was his debut, his fellow-debutant, opener Gordon Greenidge had no such issues and marked his maiden Test with innings of 93 and 107. And Chandra with his bewildering array of fizzing, bouncing deliveries could make even the most experienced of batsmen look like novices.

Now back to Kotla on a typically chilly, foggy morning in December 1974.

"Richards, usually so calm, unruffled and self-confident, approached the middle with the greatest trepidation. The easy, almost languid walk to the middle was there, but deep down his stomach churned with fear. He had decided the innings was to be the most searching examination of his ability." [From the 1984 book *Viv Richards: The Authorised Biography* with Trevor McDonald).

In the documentary *Spin v Pace* the anchor Rusi Modi, the former Test batsman says Richards initially struggled against the Indian spin trio of S. Venkataraghavan, Bishan Singh Bedi and EAS Prasanna. But where was his nemesis, Chandra? And how come Richards was playing this Test in the first place? All that will be revealed later in this chapter.

The score was 73 for three when Richards walked in nervously to join the left-hander Alvin Kallicharran at the crease. Richards knew this was a do-or-die moment in his fledgling career. One more failure and he would be out of the team for the third Test.

Having scratched around for 12 runs came one of those moments that define a Test, a series, a career, indeed cricket history.

That 'Catch'

Back to McDonald: "He got off to a very slow start, and had scored 12 when he was given the benefit of the doubt in an incident which might so easily have gone the other way, and plunged his career into a trauma of self-doubt.

Pushing forward outside the off stump, the ball went through to the keeper [Farokh Engineer]. There was an almighty shout from the bowler [Venkataraghavan], wicket keeper and nearly all the Indian players. The close fielders were particularly vociferous. Richards remains absolutely convinced that he hadn't touched the ball. But the Indian players thought otherwise, and made their views known. But the umpire was unmoved and Richards stayed, breathing an audible sigh of relief."

Look at the photo. It is now over fifty years since the incident and all the six in the photo, five players and umpire Madhav Gothoskar (now 95 years old) are thankfully still with us. The youngest is the batsman, Richards. The non-striker is Kallicharran, the bowler (and captain) Venkat, the 'keeper Engineer and the slip fielder GR Vishwanath.

Richards again in the David Foot book: "I was very nervous when I came in…There were some murmurs from the Indians afterwards. They seemed to think I was caught at the wicket when I'd scored 12. They were equally sure Keith Boyce had been caught at slip before he was off the mark. I had no doubts in my mind."

The Indians on the field and in the press box had no doubts in their mind either—that Richards had nicked it and the umpire bungled in not giving him out.

The result was one of the most devastating batting displays seen on Indian soil till date—192 not out with a deluge of fours and sixes which soared across and sometimes outside Kotla, completely deflating the Indian team as they hurtled to an innings defeat to go two-down in the series.

This is how Raju Bharatan saw it from the press box: "Was Vivian Richards guilty of gamesmanship when he stood his ground as that mighty appeal for a catch at the wicket by Engineer off Venkat went up? Richards was then 12, went on to hit an unbeaten 192 and, in between, admitted he'd got a touch and was out. Why then didn't he 'walk'? As I see it, Richards "took a chance" (in the words of Venkat) and stood there because he had no Chandra to face in that Delhi Test." ('Another Miracle…almost'; *Sportsweek Cricket Quarterly*, Jan-March 1975)

But when exactly did Richards admit he got a touch? When Bharatan writes "in between" is he hinting that the batsman confessed to being out to the Indians, or perhaps to non-striker Kallicharran and was overheard? And secondly, sitting so far away in the press box, how could Bharatan have been so certain in his judgment?

This was the first series in India in which every Test was telecast live, but only within city limits. And there were certainly no slow-mo action replays or close-ups on *Doordarshan's* rudimentary TV coverage back then. In fact this particular incident is also not available in the *Spin v Pace* documentary with the *National Films Divisions* cameras apparently failing to pick it up.

Bharatan was backed by R. Sriman in *The Times of India:* "Soon after lunch, Richards fell, or so we thought, to Venkat's wiles, but umpire Gothoskar remained unmoved to an appeal for catch behind the wicket in which almost the entire squad joined. At the end of the over, which was not a maiden, mark you, the fielders, led by Bedi, applauded genuinely, removing any impression that the chorus of appeals was a gimmick." ('West Indian batsmen skin our spinners', December 13, 1974)

Wrote Sunder Rajan in his 1975 book *India vs West Indies 1974-75:* "There was a full-throated appeal against Richards for a catch off Venkat but umpire Gothoskar was unmoved…Engineer who took the catch, and the rest stood in disbelief as the ball clearly seemed to have nicked the edge of Richards' defensive bat."

Tony Cozier was the only West Indian journalist on the tour and was a byword for fairness in his reports and radio commentary. This was his view: "The Indians were convinced that he [Richards] was caught behind the wicket cutting at Venkataraghavan when he was 12 and it might well have been an umpiring mistake. If it was, it was cruel luck for India—and a large slice of fortune for Richards, for the West Indies and, indeed, the game as a whole. **This one innings has probably been**

the launching pad for an outstanding career." [Emphasis mine. 'Spin Bogey Laid to Rest'; *Sportsweek,* December 22, 1974]

What of the others on the field, apart from the batsman himself? Engineer, Vishwanath and Kallicharran all wrote their autobiographies but none of them make a mention of this episode in their books.

But two other Indians on the spot have gone on record, umpire Gothoskar and captain and bowler Venkataraghavan. And the verdict is clear—Richards did get a touch.

In his 1992 autobiography, *The Burning Finger: An Indian Umpire Looks Back,* Gothoskar is defensive about this decision: "When Richards was on 12 there was a confident appeal for caught behind by fielders off the bowling of Prasanna [he has got the bowler's name wrong!]. A drifter, which moved outside the off stump, had possibly nicked the bat as Richards played a defensive shot. I declared him not out. If Richards had then been dismissed in the twenties or even in the fifties, the incident would have been forgotten…Even for a moment, if we assumed my decision was wrong, am I a god? Hasn't Frank Chester made mistakes? Hasn't Dickie Bird too made mistakes, as he himself would be the first to admit."

Gothoskar, one of India's leading umpires at the time, paid a price, perhaps harshly, by being dropped for the rest of the series.

This is what Venkat had to say in an interview when asked to comment on the incident: **Q:** Umpire Madhav Gothoskar not to give Viv Richards out was very crucial. You were the bowler. Tell me how did it look from your side? **A:** I thought it looked pretty obvious from our side. In fact the close in fielder, Farokh, myself and everybody else went up instantaneously. There was no question of any doubt of our mind. **Q:** He was caught cleanly? **A:** Yes, there was no question of bat-pad. If it was a bat-pad decision one can sympathise with the umpire because it can be difficult to judge. Here it was a stroke played well outside the body, and caught behind the wicket." (https://timesofindia.indiatimes. com/sports/new-zealand-in-india-2016/interviews/i-felt-bad-to-miss-more-opportunity-venkatraghavan/articleshow/10157834.cms. 'I felt bad to miss more opportunity', *timesofindia.indiatimes.com*, May 17, 2016)

So **what if** the decision had gone against Richards? To the question "It could have been a career nipped in the bud?", Venkat in the interview answered: "I don't think so. I always believe that talent cannot be suppressed. It can be delayed."

Venkat could well be right here. But even before the Test began there were dramatic events that unfolded which played a leading role in Richards' career graph.

As a backgrounder we have to go back to the first Test at Bangalore. Skipper Pataudi dislocated a finger while taking a catch and had to leave the field. Gavaskar had been appointed vice-captain before the series and took over from Pataudi. Venkat it must be remembered was Wadekar's deputy from 1971 to 1974 so this decision caused a ripple.

When Pataudi was declared unfit for the Delhi Test it was announced Gavaskar would lead in the Test in his absence. But then fate struck a cruel blow—Gavaskar had his finger broken by fast bowler Pandurang Salgaoncar in a Ranji Trophy match for Bombay against Maharashtra at Nasik between the two Tests and was thus also ruled out for the Delhi Test.

Indian cricket was already in a state of flux with four resounding defeats in a row in 1974. This is when the behind-the-scenes drama unfolded. The night before the Delhi Test, senior BCCI vice-president Ram Prakash Mehra (also president of the Delhi District Cricket Association), apparently misled by an unverified agency report, unofficially announced at a function that as the senior-most member of the side, Engineer would be the captain and congratulated him on his appointment.

Imagine everyone's shock when the next morning Venkat walked out for the toss with his counterpart Lloyd. The final decision was taken just an hour before the start of play—one can only guess as to the turmoil in the Indian dressing room, already shattered by the absence of captain Pataudi and star opener Gavaskar.

Chairman of the selectors representing South Zone was CD Gopinath. He reached Delhi late at night before the start of the Test. Like Venkat, Gopinath was also from Madras, and his role proved decisive in choosing him as captain.

Now comes the sensational twist in the story. Bedi had been omitted from the Bangalore Test ostensibly on disciplinary grounds over the trivial matter of appearing on a children's show on BBC TV during the controversial tour of England a few months earlier.

The BCCI demanded an explanation as to why he had not taken permission, Bedi refused to respond to their summons and ultimately it became a personal clash between the star left-arm bowler and Board President PR Rungta.

The action caused outrage across India with the 'No Bedi, No Test' slogans and posters echoing 'No Mushtaq [Ali], No Test' and 'No Durani, No Test' protests of earlier years that had rocked Indian cricket. Ultimately it took the intervention of the Education Ministry (then in charge of sports) to cool things down and Bedi was back for the Delhi Test.

This in turn had the selectors in a quandary as to whom to drop. With Venkat as captain and Bedi back, and one of the other two spinners having to be thus omitted, the axe fell on the unfortunate Chandra who had taken six wickets at Bangalore (as had Venkat).

The unintended consequence of all these twists and turns was that Richards was rid of his bogey man who had tormented him at Bangalore and had cast doubts into his mind as to his suitability temperamentally and technically for the cauldron of international cricket.

In the McDonald biography it was said of Chandra: "Richards began to acquire a great respect for the skill of Chandrasekhar. Asked even today whether he's ever feared any bowler in the world, the name that is spoken with a kind of reverence is that of Chandrasekhar."

Mind you, this is the same batsman who faced Dennis Lillee, Jeff Thomson, Len Pascoe and Imran Khan and others at their fiercest and fastest!

Nervous Wreck

The book was released in 1985. But even in 2015 on a visit to India, Richards reiterated in a chat with Bedi that he was "seriously intimidated as well. I was a nervous wreck, I was seriously intimidated. I could not let you guys know then," while facing the spin quartet. (www. hindustantimes.com/cricket/i-was-a-nervous-wreck-playing-indian-spinners-vivian-richards/story-0LEapBcUhymXZTGWFnMkqL. html. 'I was a nervous wreck playing Indian spinners': Vivian Richards' by Sukhwant Basra and Nilankur Das, *hindustantimes.com*, August 23, 2015).

But perhaps the most vivid description of his state of mind as he came out to bat in his debut innings is in the third of his books in 2000, *Sir Vivian: The Definitive Autobiography* (with Bob Thomas): "My legs, numb from nerves, were not working properly and as I stepped onto the big bamboo step leading from the pavilion to the outfield, I stumbled and fell right to the bottom. I picked myself up and dusted myself down but my nerves were hardly settled as firecrackers flew past me…"

In the first Test at Bridgetown, Barbados in March 1976, Chandra was brought in as soon as Richards reached the crease at the fall of the second wicket. First up was his dreaded faster one which fizzed past the startled batsman who turned round and commented to wicket-keeper Syed Kirmani: "Wow, that was faster than Thommo [Jeff Thomson], maan". Soon after he was dropped at backward short-leg and went onto reach 142. This series was just a couple of months after West Indies' traumatic tour of Australia where they were thrashed 5-1, blown away by Lillee and Thomson.

Fast forward to 1979—India were on tour in England. It would be the final series for both Chandra and Bedi. The county warm-up match against Somerset between the first Test at Edgbaston and the second at Lord's was meandering to a predictable draw. Unusually for such a low-key match, Richards, the monarch of all he surveyed at the Taunton ground, was making an appearance. He had progressed to 39 easily stroked runs when substitute fielder and Chandra's Karnataka teammate, Brijesh Patel suggested to stand-in captain (for Venkat) Vishwanath that Richards' nemesis be brought onto bowl. According to Rajan Bala in his 1993 biography of Chandra, *The Winning Hand*, "A scowl seemed to mar the normally imperious countenance of the West Indian. I later heard from the Indian wicket-keeper Surinder Khanna, that Viv had said. "What has he been brought on for? I was looking forward to a relaxed stint of batting". Sure enough, he holed out to Dilip Vengsarkar at mid-wicket. " In fact Chandra got his 'bunny' with his very first ball.

Hard as it is to believe now half a century later there was one more twist to this uncanny saga and that involved the Jamaican batsman Lawrence Rowe who had made a massive impact on his debut Test against New Zealand at Sabina, Park, Kingston, the capital of Jamaica in February 1972 with a double century and century, still a unique feat in the annals of Test cricket. Just a week earlier he had scored 227 for Jamaica in the tour game at the same venue. No wonder he was known as 'Lawrence of Jamaica' (a play on Lawrence of Arabia).

Rowe came to India with the reputation as the undisputed number one batsman in the world. Earlier that year at Bridgetown, Barbados he stroked an imperious 302 against England, the first triple ton by a West Indian since Garry Sobers' world record 365 not out against Pakistan in 1958. And in the previous Test at his pocket borough of Sabina Park he had scored 120. In fact that triple was his 11th first-class century but only his first outside Sabina Park, Kingston.

Richards on the other hand was a relative unknown from the tiny island of Antigua who at the start of the 1974-75 tour would not have fancied his chances of getting a look-in for the Tests.

Row's 302 was the first and only triple century in the entire decade of the 1970s. In fact Sobers had anointed Rowe as his right-handed successor as the greatest West Indian batsman. For Jamaicans though he was seen as the successor to the one they considered the greatest of all time, George Headley, the Atlas of West Indies cricket of the 1930s and 40s, popularly known as the 'Black Bradman'. Though back home in Kingston they referred to Don Bradman as the 'White Headley'!

Rowe's career had suffered its first major health setback when Australia toured in 1973, wrenching an ankle in the third Test at Port of Spain, Trinidad which ruled him out for the rest of the series. Later that summer in England he had to leave before the start of the three-Test series as the pulled ankle ligaments had not fully healed and he could not bat for much more than an hour without pain.

Now misfortune struck in the opening match of the tour against West Zone at Poona. Rowe was out hit wicket without scoring to Karsan Ghavri, falling on his stumps. In the second innings he managed just a single.

The caption for the photo of the ungainly dismissal in *Sportsweek* (November 17, 1974) stated: "Lawrence Rowe had difficulty in sighting the ball. He falls on his wicket trying to hook Ghavri. He consulted a Poona optometrist and was advised to have spectacles fitted. He had stayed behind in Bombay to consult a specialist who confirmed that Rowe needs to wear glasses. He will join the team in Hyderabad."

This was to be the match against South Zone a week later, the third and the final warm-up match for the tourists before the start of the series.

While the superstar Rowe failed, it was the virtually unknown Richards who made an immediate impact with the first century for the tourists at Poona.

Rowe was indeed back for the Hyderabad match. Wearing his new spectacles, he scored 15 not out. However, he was still not comfortable so flew to London to consult a renowned ophthalmic surgeon. It is a measure of the worth he was to the team that the perpetually cash-strapped West Indies cricket board paid his expenses and allowed him to return to India without sending a replacement.

According to Rowe, the problem was first picked up by team manager Gerry Alexander at a restaurant in London where they made a stopover on the way to India when he held the menu very close to his face. "With my left eye, I could only read the first two lines of the optician's chart. The right eye was 20/20", he told Dileep Premachandran. He also said: "I was more naturally talented than Viv [Richards] but he accomplished a lot more. He had a full career." ('There was no shot I couldn't play', *Cricinfo* magazine, June 2007).

Rowe failed to make it back in time for the opening Test as he was still in London being examined and so his middle-order slot was filled by Richards. But he was there in Delhi in time for the second and had a session in the nets where it was ascertained that he was not yet fully fit to play.

Captain Lloyd was now on the horns of a dilemma—should he risk a tried and tested champion bat like Rowe even if not 100 per cent ready? Or should he persist with the rooky whose nerves were shot after his traumatic experience? But when word reached that Venkat was to captain and Richards' bogey man Chandra had been dropped, Lloyd gambled on the youngster to come good at Kotla, which of course he did with a vengeance.

So the inevitable question arises, **what if** Rowe had been fit from the start of the tour? With Roy Fredericks and Gordon Greenidge opening and Kallicharran and Lloyd next, followed by wicket-keeper Deryck Murray and then the pace bowling all-rounders Bernard Julien and Keith Boyce and finally the spin bowlers, there was just one vacant spot in the middle-order.

Richards was the form batsman going into the Tests with that century against West Zone in the tour opener. And just before the second at Delhi he scored 103 not out and 53 not out against North Zone at Jullunder. Rowe on the other hand was short of match practice due to his London trip. The issue was a stye on the eyelid and so from Delhi once he failed to make into the XI, he was sent home for treatment. He was suffering from pterygium, a disease involving vision-blurring growths—this had almost completely covered his left eye and there was a risk of it obscuring vision in the right. A remedial operation damaged his eyesight; contact lenses were prescribed, but in the days before the invention of soft lenses, these caused his eyes to water profusely,

These medical details were revealed by Australian writer Gideon Haigh in an article in *Wisden Asia Cricket* ('Falling from Olympus', April 2004).

Rowe, like all leading West Indians of that era, had a stint in county cricket in the summer of 1974 leading up to India. But though he scored exactly 1,000 runs for Derbyshire it was at a disappointing average of 37.03 without a single century in 16 matches (28 innings), highest score 94. And to add to his litany of health woes, he was beset by headaches and hay fever compounded by a typically wet English summer where Derbyshire finished bottom of the county championship. The last straw though was when it was discovered he had developed an allergy, of all things for a cricketer, to grass!

All this meant he missed the inaugural Prudential World Cup in England which West Indies won and in which Richards made his mark more with his fielding than batting.

Coming back to the India series, Tony Cozier with his unique insights into the West Indian camp was emphatic in his report on the Delhi Test: "It is ironic that had Rowe not been suffering from his eyesight problems, Richards probably would have been watching these Tests [Bangalore and Delhi] from the pavilion." ('Spin Bogey Laid to Rest', *Sportsweek*, December 22, 1974).

That headline and Cozier's analysis proved premature. With Pataudi back as captain from the third Test onwards—and Chandra back in the XI too—the Indians made a stunning comeback to win the third Test at Calcutta and then draw level by winning the fourth at Madras too before succumbing at Bombay to give the visitors a hard-fought and memorable 3-2 series rubber.

Poor Venkat! From captain he was now consigned to 12th man duties at Calcutta and for the next two Tests as well. But with Chandra back in action, it was anxious times again for Richards. In the end he lost his wicket to the leg spinner only once but in the next six innings he had disappointing scores of 15, 47, 50, 2, 1 and 39 not out. His massive Delhi innings though was enough to push him up to third in the Test averages behind Lloyd and Kallicharran with 353 runs at 50.42. Then in the two Test matches on the Pakistan leg he flopped, managing only 17 runs in three innings.

Richards' and Rowe's paths and fortunes/misfortunes continued to crisscross each other throughout the 1970s in spooky and uncanny ways, throwing up enough **what if** scenarios to fill a book.

After a memorable first Prudential World Cup final in which West Indies beat Australia by 17 runs, the two teams were set to face each other in a six-Test series Down Under in the winter of 1975-76. It was billed as the world Test championship even though the first WTC final would be staged nearly 50 years after the first world ODI final. It was sure to be a treat for fans and everyone with even a faint interest in cricket tuned in to what was anticipated to be a stirring contest with brilliant batsmen and ferocious fast bowlers on both sides.

In the event it turned out to be an anti-climatic rout with West Indies crushed 5-1. The result shook West Indies cricket to the core and put Lloyd's captaincy under severe stress.

But mid-way through it could have gone either way. Australia won the opener at Brisbane by eight wickets with newly appointed captain Greg Chappell scoring a century in each innings. The tourists came storming back with a crushing innings win at Perth's lightning fast WACA pitch and it looked like the pre-series hype was well warranted. But after Australia went 2-1 up by winning the third at Melbourne by eight wickets, the wheels fell off the Windies wagon as they were crushed in the next three Tests and Australia were Test champions of the world, even if unofficially. Just the previous season they had thrashed England 4-1 at home—now they went one better.

Rowe started with a bang, 107 in the first Test—the first of his career outside West Indies—and a partnership of 198 with Alvin Kallicharran (101) in the second innings. At this stage of his career the 26-year-old's average stood at a phenomenal 70.33 with six centuries, including a triple and a double in 13 Tests. It looked like he had regained the magical form. But then he faded away with just one half century in the next five Tests. He ended the series with 270 runs at the poor average of 24.55.

For Richards, it was just the opposite. He began disappointingly, but then ended with a bang to finish with the second highest aggregate, 426 runs compared to Lloyd's 469. But after the grueling tour of India, Sri Lanka and Pakistan where he had the solitary Delhi century in seven Tests in all, Richards was still racked with self-doubt and was not even sure he would be chosen for the Australian tour.

The Good Doctor

Richards' poor run in the first four Tests saw him turn in desperation to famed sports psychologist and former Barbados fast bowler Dr. Rudi

Webster. In Richards' case it was clearly a case of mind over matter. He wrote in the *Sir Vivian* autobiography: "I had problems early on [in the series] and had scores of 0, 12 and 12. It created some doubts in my own mind as to my own abilities at this rarefied level; in fact, it was panic stations…We discovered through discussions I wasn't concentrating the way I should have been when I reached a certain stage of my innings. Then it was a question of discussing how I could do so and taking it onto another level, going forward step by step."

Webster said in an interview with Sidhartha Vaidyanathan in *Cricinfo* magazine ('Veeru's Return Ticket', August 2006): "Most of the work I did with Viv was related to watching the ball and getting into position. I showed Viv how to lower his arousal level and taught him how to increase his confidence."

That was just what the doctor ordered. The tour selectors were looking for an opener to replace Greenidge who had lost form and confidence and Richards stepped forward to partner Fredericks. He felt opening in the tour games would give him more time at the crease in preparation for the Tests.

Lloyd agreed, but **what if** he had not chosen Richards to open in the match against Tasmania at Hobart after the fourth Test at Sydney, won by the hosts by seven wickets to go 3-1 up in the series? Richards responded with scores of 160 and 107 not out and this brought back a rush of confidence, bolstered by sessions with Webster.

The first four Tests brought Richards only 147 runs from seven innings. Once again his Test future was teetering on the edge before that Hobart performance and his promotion to opening the innings with Fredericks in the last two Tests came as a shot in the arm. Opening gave Richards less time to brood in the dressing room while awaiting his turn to bat in the middle order.

As Webster said in the *Cricinfo* interview:"Like golf, cricket goes on for a long time and there are many periods of inactivity. So the mind has a lot of time to get up to mischief…In those early days, Viv was very nervous, particularly while waiting his turn to bat. Clive Lloyd recognised this problem and promoted him in the batting order to open the innings. This move helped to relieve some of the pressure." [The latter part of this quote is from an interview with Webster by Rahul Bhattacharya in *Wisden Asia Cricket* March 2003 issue headlined 'The art of arousal')

The combined wisdom of Webster and Lloyd saw Richards reel off scores of 30, 101, 50 and 98 in the fifth and sixth Tests as he took on the fiery fast bowling head on. West Indies slid from defeat to defeat and ended the series in disarray. But while Lloyd's captaincy was under threat, Richards' career got a second life.

But there was hardly any breathing space for the beleaguered Caribs as within less than a month they plunged straight into a four-Test series against India at home.

India under new captain Bedi had just drawn a three-Test series 1-1 in New Zealand and now the microscope was on Lloyd's leadership. He could not under any circumstances afford another slip-up. But while Lloyd might have thought this would be a relatively easy assignment, it proved to be both hard-fought and stormy. West Indies won 2-1, but it was not a cakewalk by any means (see next chapter for more details).

Lucky Escapes

For Richards, playing a home series for the first time after three abroad, it was the best yet of his young career which was still not two years old. Having survived—just about—the trial by fire of speed Down Under, he now established supremacy over the world's best spin bowling attack with centuries in each of the first three Tests and 64 in the fourth and final.

Now back to his usual middle-order slot, Richards easily topped the averages with 556 runs from six innings at 92.66. It was Rowe who was pushed up the order to open with Fredericks, without success though with a top score of 47 from six innings.

But **what if** he had not been given reprieves, via missed catches and stumpings by the hapless wicket-keeper Syed Kirmani in just the latter's second series? How differently things may have turned out.

Kirmani had served a long apprenticeship under both P. Krishnamurthy and Engineer starting with the 1971 England tour. In New Zealand just before the West Indies series he put on an excellent show, even equaling the world record for most wicket-keeper dismissals in an innings (6; one stumping, five catches) in the second Test at Christchurch, just the second Test of his career.

In West Indies though his form fell to pieces with Venkat being the unfortunate bowler to suffer the most at the hands of the rookie 'keeper.

Wrote Cozier: "Wicketkeeper Kirmani had a very unfortunate series, missing some of the easiest stumpings and catches that have ever come his way. It was nevertheless obvious that this young man has kept in better fashion in the past—and is capable of doing so in the future as well. The man who profited most from Kirmani's lapses was the West Indian main run getter Vivian Richards who was dropped at least once by Kirmani in all his major knocks. Richards, however emerged as a batsman of the highest class..."('A near miracle', *Sportsweek's World of Cricket*, April-June 1976):

Without going into the gory details of each miss, one photo published in *Sportsweek* (April 18, 1976) summed up Richards' good luck and Kirmani's poor form best (or worst). It showed Richards way out of his crease looking back helplessly even as the wicket-keeper fumbles with the ball slipping out of his big gloves. This was in the second Test at Port of Spain and the hapless bowler was of course Venkat. The batsman was on 83 and went onto score 130.

Prasanna in his 1977 autobiography *One More Over* expressed his dismay: "In the second Test at Port of Spain (Trinidad) we should have won. But poor catching and some shoddy wicket-keeping by Kirmani let us down. I couldn't believe it was the same Kirmani who had done such a wonderful job in New Zealand. Venkat bowled magnificently, but was terribly unlucky."

Kishore Bhimani was reporting the series for *The Statesman* daily of Calcutta. In his 1976 book *West Indies '76: India's Caribbean Adventure*, he wrote of the incident: "After the [lunch] break, India should have had a vital breakthrough. As Richards and [Deryck] Murray were settling down to some sensible batting, taking the score to 143 for 4, Richards once more decided to test the alertness of wicketkeeper Kirmani. After tormenting the burly Antiguan batsman with some complicated stuff, Venkat finally lured Richards into indiscretion as the batsman strode three paces down the track to meet one that straightened. Viv failed to make contact and appeared resigned to being stumped. Incredibly, Kirmani fumbled, lost the ball in his pads and, unbelievably, with a grin of relief on his face, Richards hastened back to his crease." He was eventually bowled by Bedi at 212 for 6 having scored 130.

So just as the turn of events in Indian cricket—both on and off field—helped Richards overcome his jitters in just his second Test in December 1974 with that amazing knock, here too it was against India that he rode his luck and finally established himself in the strong West Indies batting lineup, a spot he would never relinquish till his retirement in 1991.

In fact 1976 turned out to be a landmark year for the legend. Starting with the fourth Test at Sydney and ending with the fifth against England at The Oval, Richards scored a world record 1,710 runs for the calendar year in 11 Test matches (19 innings) averaging 90 with seven centuries including two doubles in England, ending the year with his highest Test score of 291 at The Oval in August. It was a record that stood for 30 years till it was erased by Pakistan's Mohammad Yousuf (formerly Yousuf Yohanna) with 1,788 runs also in 11 Tests in 2006.

That series in England finally established him as a superstar with 829 runs from four Tests, missing one due to an illness. England under Tony Greig were crushed 3-0 under the batting might of Richards and his merry men and the fast bowling battery of Holding, Roberts and Wayne Daniel. It was the most runs in a Test series in England since Don Bradman's 974 in 1930 which is seemingly unbreakable.

As for Rowe, kept out by the terrific form all tour by the other batsman, he played just the fourth and fifth and final Tests, doing reasonably well with scores of 50, 6 and 70.

Rowe's Woes and WSC

There was no end to Rowe's injury woes. He broke a finger while fielding in Jamaica's second Shell Shield match of the domestic season against Trinidad and Tobago in early January 1977 and had to sit out the entire year. That same year the news of Kerry Packer's breakaway World Series Cricket in which over 50 of the world's best cricketers signed up rocked the cricket world. Rowe joined the cream of the West Indies crop as Packer fielded three full international teams—WSC Australia, WSC West Indies and the World XI.

In the second and final season (1978-79) Rowe scored an innings (175) of incandescent brilliance against the Australians in Melbourne which brought back nostalgic memories of his glory days and proved he still had that magic touch despite all his setbacks. He was wearing a new contact lens in his left eye and batted with supreme confidence for 404 minutes, stroking 24 crisply struck fours. In the previous match against the World XI he had struck form with 85.

His 175 won rave reviews from everyone who witnessed it. WSC had the best fast bowlers on the planet and the greatest batsmen too. The likes of Viv Richards, Barry Richards, Greg Chappell, Clive Lloyd, Majid Khan, Zaheer Abbas and others all had their moments with brilliant displays. But it was universally acknowledged that Rowe's 175 topped them all.

In the *West Indies Cricket Annual* 1979 this sentence stood out for me in the match report: "…[the innings] convinced everyone who saw it live or via television of his class." The headline in the Melbourne *Age* daily was 'Rowe the Greatest West Indian: Sobers."

Sobers was a consultant to Packer for recruiting West Indian players and had convinced the TV magnate to sign Rowe despite his lack of recent form.

When he was finally out to left-arm spinner Ray Bright, the crowd at Melbourne's VFL Park gave him a standing ovation and even that fierce competitor Dennis Lillee was moved to give him a pat on his back as Rowe walked off the park, the applause ringing in his ears.

Rowe in fact etched a bit of his own WSC history. In the very last match before Packer wound up his enterprise, Rowe scored the last century for the West Indians in their 'Supertest' against the Australians, at St. John's, Antigua in April 1979.

Another twist: In the first WSC season Richards topped the averages in the 'Supetests' with Rowe right down the list; in the second it was Rowe who was on top while Richards had a miserable season.

Rowe's rotten luck continued on his fourth and last tour to England in 1980—he dislocated a shoulder and took no part in the Test matches. His last Test series had come in New Zealand in February 1980 on West Indies' stormy tour which they lost 1-0 under highly controversial circumstances. In the second Test at Christchurch—the penultimate of his career—Rowe scored the seventh century and final century in his career lasting only 30 Tests.

Discarded, despondent and distressed, in December 1982 he signed up as captain of the rebel West Indies team to tour Apartheid South Africa. If Packer's WSC hit the cricket world like an earthquake, a team of West Indians touring South Africa hit it like a tsunami. Now ostracized in his native Jamaica, Rowe moved to Miami, Florida in the United States where many West Indian ex-cricketers reside. But his debut world record remains untouched after all these years and the memory of his silken stroke-play undimmed for all those privileged to have seen him in his prime.

Postscript One: Early in the chapter I described the way the career paths and fortunes/misfortunes of Richards and Rowe crisscrossed each other as "spooky and uncanny". How is this for spooky and uncanny? In 1984 Richards suffered from the exact same pterygium eye ailment as Rowe though he avoided surgery thanks to a local herbal remedy. And like Rowe he also suffered from hay fever. This is revealed in his book with Bob Thomas.

Postscript Two: The focus of this book is on Indian cricket and this chapter deals with two West Indian cricketers. So how come? Reason: it was on the 1974-75 tour of India that their careers took dramatic turns and this continued when India toured West Indies in 1976.

CHAPTER EIGHT

Gone with the Windies Part II

More Tales from the Caribbean

"Gentlemen, I gave you 400 runs to bowl at and you failed to bowl out the opposition. How many runs must I give you in the future to make sure you get the wickets?"

It was a rhetorical question at best posed by West Indies' captain Clive Lloyd at the end of the third Test at Queen's Park Oval, Port of Spain, Trinidad in April 1976 to Imtiaz Ali, Albert Padmore (both on debut) and Raphick Jumadeen. But they had no answer, in any case. Between the three of them they had bowled 167 overs over two innings for the paltry return of five wickets against India who had just set the world record for the highest fourth innings total to win a Test match, finishing on 406 for four. That record would stand for 27 years. It meant the four-Test series was now level at 1-1 with one to go.

Only once before in the 99 years of Test cricket till then had a team scored over 400 to win and that was by Don Bradman's 'Invincibles' on their all-conquering tour of England in 1948.

Lloyd's ominous words effectively sounded the death knell for spin bowling in West Indies for the foreseeable future and would unleash on an unsuspecting world the spectre of not three but four fast bowlers bowling in tandem and smashing stumps and bones.

The next Test at Sabina Park, Kingston, Jamaica would see only Jumadeen survive the chop as Lloyd chose the four-man pace attack of Michael Holding, Wayne Daniel, Vanburn Holder and Bernard Julian which set the template for West Indies cricket. Lloyd and his all-conquering men were however only warming up.

But we are getting ahead of ourselves. The seed of the idea was placed in Lloyd's mind after the fearful hammering his team received in Australia in 1975-76 in what was billed as the unofficial Test championship of the world but which fizzled into a no-contest. Up against the relentless fast bowling of Dennis Lillee and Jeff Thomson, backed by the swing of Gary Gilmour and Max Walker, Australia inflicted a fearful 5-1 drubbing on the chastened West Indians.

In the 1985 book *Clive Lloyd: The Authorised Biography* from which the quote at the start of this chapter is taken, Lloyd's biographer Trevor McDonald writes that after the Port of Spain Test: "Lloyd swore that he would never again be let down by spinners. On wickets fast and slow, he would employ pace. Doing away with spinners would enable him to play four fast bowlers instead of two. His mind had been made up. His distrust of spinners dovetailed neatly with his confidence about the effectiveness of fast bowling."

But it was due to a freak of nature, so to speak that the third Test was played at Port of Spain at all. Rain played a part in this as it did in the second Test at the same venue.

Fresh—or perhaps not—from their three-Test series in New Zealand, the Indians endured a 62-hour journey and were thoroughly jet-lagged by the time they reached the Caribbean. After two warm-up games they went into the first Test at Bridgetown, Barbados and were soundly beaten in three days by an innings and 97 runs.

But their spirits were lifted when the action shifted to Trinidad. With the large Indian-origin population always backing them enthusiastically and the pitch at the Queen's Park Oval being spin friendly, Port of Spain was like a home-away-from-home for the tourists. This is where after all India had recorded their first victory on West Indian soil in the second Test of the 1971 series which helped them win their maiden series 1-0 (Chapter 6). And in the fifth and final Test of that series at the same ground, Sunil Gavaskar made cricket history with a century and double century in the same match.

That same 1971 series had started off in dramatic fashion at Kingston, Jamaica with West Indies forced to follow on for the first time in 24 Tests against India going back to 1948-49. It was a humiliation they never recovered from for the rest of the series and came about even though India led by 170 runs and not 200, the minimum lead required to enforce the follow-on. That was because no play was possible on the opening day due to rain and thus the Test was reduced to four days and the lead requirement for the follow-on was cut to 150 runs.

Now five years later history repeated itself in the second Test, but with a twist. The first day's play was also washed out without a ball bowled. But this time it backfired on the tourists who bounced back bravely from the Barbados beating.

The Test was drawn but with a few more hours of play it could have so easily gone India's way. So how did India lose the golden chance to bounce back?

This was a match in which India were on top right from Day One, or rather Day Two in this case. But there were crucial blunders in the field that let the home side off the hook.

The first miss was the fumbled stumping by Syed Kirmani off S. Venkataraghavan when Richards was on 83 (See Chapter 7). So **what if** Kirmani had completed the easy chance?

The total at that stage was 143 for 4 and with his dismissal the tail would have been exposed and it is doubtful if the total would have crossed 175-180. Richards went onto his second century in the series and carried the Windies' batting on his broad shoulders—130 out of 241. But crucially in a match reduced to four days and with the spinners right on top, precious time would have been saved as well as Richards ground out his innings over a tad under five hours, slow by his standards.

After the opening bowlers Madan Lal and Mohinder Amaranth removed openers Roy Fredericks and Lawrence Roy for four runs between them, the spin trio of BS Chandrasekhar, captain Bishan Bedi and Venkat took control, and how.

Alvin Kallicharran and Lloyd were both dismissed cheaply and the hosts were struggling at 52 for four. Richards, following his 142 in the first Test, found himself tied down by the master spinners. It took him more than two hours to reach 50 and the Windies' batting would have collapsed if not for his partnership of 122 with wicket-keeper Deryck Murray (46). Richards was sixth out, bowled by Bedi, one of his five wickets and the Indians had done a splendid job in bowling out their opponents for a sub-par total.

With Gavaskar and Brijesh Patel both scoring centuries, Bedi declared at 402 for 5, giving India a substantial lead. But time was as much a factor as runs with the match reduced to four days and this is where the batting of Patel and Madan Lal could be faulted.

The pair added 72 runs after the departure of Gavaskar at 330 for four 35 minutes after lunch on the fourth day, following a double century stand with Patel. At that stage India were 89 runs ahead and quick scoring was the need of the hour. But as he approached his maiden Test century, Patel allowed his nerves to get the better of him and slowed down. Normally attacking batsmen by nature, the two scored their runs in two hours just when they should have stepped on the accelerator. This meant the declaration was delayed till 70 minutes before stumps in which Windies lost the wicket of Fredericks.

Kishore Bhimani was one of three Indian reporters on the tour, the other two being KN Prabhu and the England-based Dicky Rutnagur. This is how Bhimani described the partnership between Patel and Madan Lal in his book *West Indies'76: India's Caribbean Adventure:* " ...Patel appeared dazzled by the sudden realization that he was approaching his century. Madanlal just could not get going…the need of the moment was some quick runs."

Tony Cozier put it this way in *West Indies Cricket Annual* 1976: "It was now that Patel and Madanlal needed to hurry the scoring but they were kept on tight rein by steady West Indian bowling, defensive field placing and a pitch of uneven bounce. Yet they did not even appear to try to get on with things."

Bhimani wrote he was expecting a declaration to come around tea on the penultimate day. "But at this crucial juncture, the scoring rate fell so badly that all Bedi's plans must have gone somewhat awry. Patel was so obviously nervous in his nineties, that he played with embarrassing hesitance and Madan kept him company with even more painstaking strokes. How we could have done with some casual, carefree batting!"

At tea with the total on 363 for 5, Patel was batting two short of 100. Bedi no doubt gave the two a shellacking during the break as they now added quick runs and the declaration came with the lead reading 161 runs.

But **what if** those two hours had not been squandered? Just how crucial they were was evident on the final day as the spinners turned on the screws, chipping away in a desperate bid to close out the Test and square the series.

Wrote Brunnel Jones in *Indian Cricket 1976*: "It was a long and tortuous day for the Caribbean batsmen. The web of spin was tight all day and like the spider, the Indian spinners netted their victims one by one."

West Indies started the final day on 29 for one with one aim in mind—bat out time for a draw; there was no other option. When Richards (20) was run out, half the side had been sent back for 137, still 24 runs behind and three hours play remained. Now the Indian bowlers were on top, pressing hard for victory.

Captain Lloyd was holding the fort. But his escape at 113 for four with his own score on 27, just after the dismissal of Rowe was what was seen as the moment the hosts were let off the hook.

Unfortunately it was the two best fielders in the side who bungled. Substitute Eknath Solkar was on the field for just one over as Chandra had to replace his bootlace. Lloyd went for a massive drive off the luckless Venkat, hit against the spin and the ball spiraled in a gentle loop to mid-off where Solkar waited for the easiest of catches. Suddenly, Patel sprinted across from extra-cover, got his hands to the ball, collided heavily with Solkar and spilled it. "If ever a catch cost a victory this was it" wrote Cozier. He added: "this was a match which India richly deserved to win and should have. They were the better team throughout."

Even at tea India looked to be moving towards a sensational victory with Windies 171 for 5, just ten runs ahead. Now Bedi struck three quick blows, dismissing Lloyd, Murray and Holford without conceding a run and at 194 for 8 the lead was just 33 with 23 overs still left in the day.

Roberts and Julian hung on grimly, the former twice being given the benefit of the doubt by the umpires, first for lbw, then for a catch—for which the Indian fielders had no doubt at all. With seven overs remaining and the lead now 54 and the ninth wicket pair hanging on grimly, Bedi signaled to the umpires that there was no reason to complete the 20 mandatory overs.

The dejected Indians left the ground with their heads hung low, tormented by **what ifs** galore. But their despondency would change to elation just nine days later as they found themselves back at their favourite venue outside of India. But how and why?

Bucket loads of Rain

It was rain again, this time bucket loads in Georgetown, Guyana turning the Bourda Oval into a veritable lake. Bhimani gave a vivid picture of the scene in his tour book in the chapter titled 'Cricketless in Guyana'. Even as the three Indian journalists were being driven at night from the airport to their hotel, he wrote "the clouds opened up and sheets of rain, the likes of which I, for one, had never seen before or since, began to turn the narrow road into a death trap…"

Mind you, Bhimani lived in Calcutta where the monsoon rain could be pretty heavy. But this was something else in the only country in South America that is part of the Test cricket map.

The first concern was the tour game against Guyana to start on April 1 which was due to be the swansong for the 41-year-old master off spinner Lance Gibbs who in the Australia series had become the holder of the world Test wicket record. Gibbs, cousin of the West Indian captain, was named captain of Guyana though the West Indian selectors at the start of the series had decided to put him out to pasture and go for young blood, much to the relief of the Indians who had a poor record against Gibbs.

With the rain being incessant it was initially announced the four-day match would be delayed by a day or two. A visit to the venue provided a startling sight—half of it was under water! The cancellation of the tour game was now a formality as the focus shifted to getting the ground ready for the third Test due to begin on April 7. Desperate attempts were made to pump the water out of the ground but the rain was so relentless and heavy that talks began to swap Tests with Kingston, Jamaica, the venue of the fourth and final Test. That offer was flatly turned down.

The turbulent Demerara River which posed a constant threat to Georgetown was swollen and ready to burst its banks. There was a nine-foot high sea wall which had been built to keep the water from entering the capital located below sea level. Such was the threat of flooding, all houses along the sea face were built on stilts without ground floors, even the fancy penthouses.

Finally the inevitable dawned. Despite the heroic efforts of the ground staff, there was no let up in the turbulent weather and the difficult decision was made to shift the venue of the third Test back to Port of Spain. This was a case of history repeating itself, though under different circumstances for when India toured in 1962 the Georgetown Test was also cancelled due to civil unrest.

The Indian team were obviously delighted with the turn of events. Wrote GR Vishwanath in his 2022 autobiography *Wrist Assured*: "As we boarded the aircraft, I could see the joy and unexpected bonus of playing a second successive Test at the Queen's Park Oval. The backing of the Indian population in Port of Spain, and our record at the ground, convinced us that we could pull off something special. The conviction wavered for four days. Then came deliverance."

Lloyd had only gone in with one specialist spin bowler in the second Test, Jumadeen as well as veteran all-rounder David Holford. Now when the teams were back at the same venue, it was decided to rest Roberts who was burned out after the strenuous Australian tour where he was the spearhead and who had proven both ineffective and uninterested on the slow turner in the second Test. Holford too was dropped.

This is when the decision was taken to bring in three specialist spinners for the first and last time under Lloyd's captaincy. But without the veteran Gibbs, who was match fit and raring to go, the selectors were forced to bring in the two debutants. Gibbs was bitter at being ignored. When the Indians toured in 1971 it was also decided to sideline him in place of Trinidad off spinner Jack Noreiga, a move which back then too the Indians were quietly pleased about.

There was a third century on the trot by Richards (177) and once again he was lucky, dropped by Kirmani when on 72. This was getting to be a habit and one that did not please Bedi and his bowlers. That innings constituted nearly half the total of 359. India responded with a meek 228, Holding taking his first 5-wicket haul in Tests.

Once Kallicharran reached his first century of the series, Lloyd declared at 271 for six. The target was 403 runs in 535 minutes, surely too high a mountain to climb for any side, let alone the Indians in Lloyd's estimation. But that mountain was indeed conquered and with centuries by Gavaskar and Vishwanath and Amarnath playing the sheet anchor with a priceless 85, the headline to Cozier's report in *The Cricketer* (June 1976) said it all: 'India Scale Test Cricket's Mount Everest.'

Lloyd had already been announced as captain for the tour to England later that summer. But the knives were out for him. He now made the fateful decision for the fourth and final Test at Kingston to focus on pace bowling.

But **what if** the venue had not been switched from the Bourda Oval in Georgetown, Guyana back to the Queen's Park Oval at Port of Spain, Trinidad because of rain? Chances are the series would have been sealed there and then in West Indies' favour and thus Lloyd would not have needed to take recourse to the drastic tactics at Kingston.

The Bloodbath

Now came one of the most controversial matches in cricket history, what has come to be known in India as the 'Bloodbath at Kingston', though Lloyd and his merry men did not quite see it that way. Three Indian batsmen were injured by the bouncer and beamer barrage including opener Aunshuman Gaekwad who suffered a life threatening injury after being struck on the left ear by a Holding thunderbolt.

Gaekwad, who passed away in September 2024, top scored with a courageous 81 and was hit all over the body before the final blow, vividly described in blood-curdling detail in his 2023 autobiography *Guts Amidst Bloodbath: The Aunshuman Gaekwad Narrative* with Aditya Bhushan.

Bedi complained to the umpires Ralph Gosein and Douglas Sang Hue, the most experienced in the region, citing Law 46 and its notes ("the persistent bowling of fast short-pitched balls at the batsman is "unfair" if, in the opinion of the umpire at the bowler's end, it constitutes a systematic attempt at intimidation.")

Sang Hue's reply was "Mr. Captain, you will leave tomorrow. But we live here," while Gosein merely laughed it off. The signal was clear—there was no way an umpire in West Indies could intervene when such an act could and often did spark a riot, especially since Holding was the local lad and the crowd had been egging him on by calling for him to kill the Indians. On the rest day manager Polly Umrigar and Bedi held a press conference where they described the events as a "war" rather than a cricket match.

With the captain and Chandra injured while fielding, the Indian second innings came to a close at 97 for 5, just 13 runs ahead as five of the players were unable to bat. Bedi made it clear this was no declaration but the signals from the Indian camp were loud and clear.

Lloyd got what he wanted—a series win by hook-or-by-crook. The events went largely unnoticed in an era where the media was not omnipresent as it is today. But the tactics finally hit the headlines just three months later in the third Test at Old Trafford, Manchester when Holding, Roberts and Daniel gave a fearful battering to England's veteran openers John Edrich and Brian Close—and now the umpires did step in. Lloyd's comments this time, with the English media up in arms were placatory: "our boys got a bit carried away". At Kingston Lloyd, Richards, and others had been scornful and insulting of the Indians' protests, though Holding to his credit in his two books expressed regret.

The events at Sabina Park and Old Trafford should have woken up the authorities and they did. But it was many years later that they eventually led to the appointment of neutral umpires and the Match Referee for all international matches as well the restriction of two bouncers per over. Also, these events and the serious injury to Australian batsman David Hookes struck by a Roberts bouncer in the first season of WSC (1977-78) finally saw the advent of protective helmets for batsmen under fire.

What if it had not rained, which resulted in the Georgetown Test being shifted back to Port of Spain? And **what if** India had not stunned one and all by thus winning the third Test, pushing Lloyd to enforce dangerous and blatantly unfair tactics in the decider? Would all these changes have eventually come into effect? Most probably they would have. But Bedi's protests certainly helped in nudging the authorities into action.

Talking about the authorities, immediately following the Old Trafford Test, the normally moribund ICC sprung into action, issuing statements at its annual meeting at Lord's in July condemning intimidatory bowling and announced support for umpires in all countries in enforcing Law 46 and its notes The use of 'beamers' was also condemned.

This reaction was solely due to what was witnessed on English soil where the media and public outcry forced the hand of the ICC. What happened months earlier in Jamaica had been shrugged off as England (and Australia) still ruled the cricket world and the English media enjoyed huge clout back then.

But at the end of the day, it was Bedi's bold stance in taking a stand on the spirit of the game that needs to be lauded and acknowledged. As for West Indies, with their four-pronged fast bowling attack and an array of brilliant batsmen, they lost just one Test series when at full strength from 1976 to 1995. But their decline has been rapid over the last 25 years.

The Domino Effect

The Domino Effect—the phenomenon where one dramatic event leads to another and another—began at Georgetown, Guyana on

March 21, 1989. It set in motion events over the next ten months that would make this period one of the most turbulent in Indian cricket history with three captains, bans, court verdicts, defeats, wins (a few) and some important draws too. Chaos, turmoil, scandals, sackings, accusations, counter-accusations…you name it, they were all out in the open.

It was the fifth and final ODI and West Indies had already taken the series 4-0. After piling up 289 for two (in 43.5 overs), the Windies mean machine was in full swing. Openers Arun Lal and K. Srikkanth were up against the thunderbolts of Ian Bishop, Curtly Ambrose, Courtney Walsh and Eldine Baptiste and were on a hiding-to-nothing.

Arun Lal was the first to go with the total at ten, a victim of Bishop. Then the new fast bowling sensation struck again—and how. Vice-captain to Dilip Vengsarkar, Srikkanth was having a miserable run in the ODIs. He had reached 17 when a kicking delivery from Bishop fractured his left forearm above the wrist. With the four-Test series to follow, it was goodbye Srikkanth for the rest of the tour.

But why was this moment pivotal in the months ahead and indeed in the history of Indian cricket? That we shall soon discover.

After the whitewash in the ODIs, the Indians fared no better in the Test series. Only the rain-ruined first Test at Georgetown was drawn with barely two days play possible. Sanjay Manjrekar alone among the hapless Indian batsman emerged with a degree of credit, topping the aggregates and averages with 200 runs at 33.33. The captain had a shocker, averaging 18.33 with just one half-century. All were swept aside by the furious onslaught unleashed by Bishop, Walsh, Ambrose and Malcolm Marshall.

All the more surprising then that the captain would condemn his batsmen in a shocking interview to Mudar Patherya of the erstwhile Calcutta-based weekly *Sportsworld*, going as far as accusing his team-mates of running away from fast bowling. Headlined 'Why We Lost', it appeared in the issue of March 17, 1989.

The most critical comments were highlighted in the magazine: "Some of the Indian batsmen in the front order batted with the same sort of approach to fast bowling as Madan Lal's in the seventies. They ran away from the fast bowling. It was a shame to see this happening in international cricket. If they are scared of a cricket ball, they should never play the game again."

Also: "You can't do a thing if a chap is running away from the fast bowling to square leg, right in the middle of a Test match. All these players, nursed on pitches in India where the balls don't rise above the knee are tigers until they step outside the country. As soon as they are selected, for an overseas tour, they run for cover."

And perhaps the most telling: "They were those who wanted to avoid playing…Of the 17 touring members in the West Indies I had the option of choosing from only 11 or 12 on most occasions. There were some from the other five who faked muscle pulls before Test matches."

This was no knee-jerk, spur-of-the-of-moment outburst by a frustrated and angry captain. Patherya showed the transcripts to the captain, so stunned was he by the outburst. After making some changes, Vengsarkar gave the go ahead for publication. This is narrated by Harsha Bhogle in *Azhar: The Authorized Biography of Mohammad Azharuddin.*

The fallout was immediate. The players—minus the injured Srikkanth and three others— were in the United States playing a series of unauthorized exhibition matches when news of the interview reached them. It caused great disquiet that their captain had hung his own team out to dry. News travelled slowly those days; imagine the outrage if it had happened in today's Social Media-driven age.

Ever since winning the World Cup in 1983 the value of Indian cricketers had risen sky-high. They were suddenly in demand and naturally enough as professionals were keen on cashing in on this new found popularity. The US and Canada trips where they were handsomely paid to play a bunch of meaningless matches did not go down well with the BCCI. The Vengsarkar interview added to their ire.

It all culminated in a perfect storm with the Board claiming the players had violated terms of their contract in playing privately organized matches not authorized by the BCCI. The five-man disciplinary committee announced on August 6 bans on six of the senior players—the captain, Ravi Shastri, Azharuddin, Kapil Dev, Arun Lal and Kiran More. The punishment: no cricket, either international or domestic for 12 months, plus monetary fines. The younger players (M. Venkatramana, Sanjay Manjrekar, Sanjeev Sharma, Robin Singh and Narendra Hirwani) were let off with smaller fines and no ban as the committee claimed they had been misled by the seniors.

The players now decided to revive the long-defunct Players' Association and sought legal opinion on the contracts and also their bans. And sure enough, just 40 days later, Justice ES Venkataramaiah of the Supreme Court, no less, came down on the side of the players. That was remarkably quick considering how slowly the wheels of justice turn in India. The ban was immediately lifted.

But there was another reason behind the hurried lifting of the ban. The government as part of its elaborate celebrations for the birth centenary of Jawaharlal Nehru (his grandson Rajiv Gandhi was the Prime Minister) was planning to stage a tournament on the lines of the World Cup with all the top teams around the world participating. There was no way India could field a team sans Kapil Dev & Co. The MRF World Series for the Jawaharlal Nehru Cup staged in October 1989 saw England, West Indies, Pakistan, Sri Lanka, Pakistan apart from the hosts battling it out. India were beaten by West Indies in the semifinal and Imran Khan led Pakistan to victory in the final at Eden Gardens.

Unsurprisingly, captain Vengsarkar got the axe and Srikkanth was chosen to lead. But why Srikkanth and not Shastri who had led India to victory in the fourth and final Test v West Indies in Madras in January 1988 in place of the injured Vengsarkar?

For one thing, Srikkanth was vice-captain on the West Indies tour which was ended prematurely for him by Bishop. But the other factor was Shastri also being one of the originally banned senior six.

So **what if** Srikkanth had not been injured in the Georgetown ODI which preceded the Test series? There is no way to predict how his batting would have held up against the awesome fast bowling attack— he had already flopped in the ODI series. But one thing for sure: he would have been a star attraction of the North American jamboree.

It's anyone's guess then who would have replaced Vengsarkar in the hot seat. He had already earned a bad boy image by ignoring the diktat against players attaching their names to syndicated columns, thus getting a six-month ban at the end of the home series against West Indies in 1987-88. And there was no way any court of law could interfere with the selection process.

After Srikkanth's surprise appointment, Vengsarkar played under his captaincy both in the Nehru Cup and the Sharjah three-nation tournament which preceded it. But he made himself unavailable for the four-Test series that followed in Pakistan at the fag-end of 1989, saying he was not in the right frame of mind to tour. This was to be Srikkanth's maiden Test series in charge and a trial by fire for any Indian captain, let alone a new one.

But the lingering effects of the display of player-power and the tussle with officialdom was hanging like a cloud over Indian cricket and manifested itself in the run-up to the tour.

This time the confrontation centred round the contracts which the team were very unhappy about as they felt it restricted their earning rights. This issue went back two years to right before the start of the 1987 Reliance World Cup. The day before the opening ceremony the team returned their contracts unsigned and with three clauses deleted, those pertaining to logos, participation in private tournaments and contributing columns to the media, all future flashpoints.

Their demands for extra match fees had not been met. In protest, the players with Srikkanth taking the lead as captain, refused to accept any remuneration for the tour as a matter of principle. This after the Board announced it was ready to send an alternate team to Pakistan with Sandeep Patil as captain if they did not sign. However, the newcomers to the team, including Sachin Tendulkar were exempted from the protest as they were at the start of their careers.

After all that tension, India under Srikkanth did well to draw all four Tests, especially considering India's poor track record in Pakistan since the late 1970s. The real game-changer though was Pakistan captain Imran Khan's bold decision to bring in two English umpires, John Hampshire and John Holder as neutrals for the entire series. That took the tension out of umpiring decisions which had often been contentious, though the volatile home crowds did not appreciate the English pair.

Imran had earlier brought in two Indian umpires as neutral for the second and third Tests of the home series against West Indies in 1986.

The Hindu's famed cricket correspondent R. Mohan went so far in *Indian Cricket* 1990 as to write: "The 'Men of the Series' were not players on either side. They were umpires. John Hampshire and John Holder gave a whole new twist to the continuum drama of Indo-Pak cricket. Never in its 38-year history had a Test series between the subcontinental neighbors passed off so peacefully. (Headlined 'The success of neutral umpiring')

After his batting slump in the Caribbean, Azhar the night before the first Test at Karachi was told that he would not be in the playing XI the next morning. It was the first time since he had made such a sensational debut in 1984-85 and after 30 Tests that he found himself dropped.

But the next morning fate had its say. Raman Lamba, who was to replace Azhar in the side, announced he had a fractured finger and dropped out. Azhar was back and grabbed the opportunity with both hands, at least while fielding at slip to equal the world record of five catches in an innings, some quite brilliant. With the bat he scored 35 in both innings, enough to retain his place for the second Test at Faisalabad and here his century cemented his place in the side.

The captain however was struggling, finishing with 97 runs in seven innings and averaging a miserable 13.85, even worse than that of the previous captain in West Indies.

So what was the fallout? Sure enough, Srikkanth after just one series in charge was also axed and replaced by Azhar for the tour of New Zealand in early 1990, thus continuing Pakistan's reputation back then as the graveyard of Indian captains.

That meant India would have its third captain in three successive Test series all in the span of less than one year. Azhar's reign was by far the longest—and most controversial—of the three.

But **what if** Lamba had not declared himself unfit on the morning of the Karachi Test, allowing Azhar a lifeline to salvage his floundering career? Srikkanth's fate was practically sealed even before the Pakistan tour began due to his role in the contracts issue. So who then would the selectors have chosen to replace him as the new captain? Your guess is as good as mine!

CHAPTER NINE

Winning Changes Everything

From 1983 to 2007

It was Saturday, 15 March 1975. My elder brother and I rushed home from our school in Kidderpore, Calcutta to catch the final minutes of the final between India and Pakistan in the World Cup hockey at Kuala Lumpur, Malaysia. We had caught snatches on transistors in the tram on the way home and celebrated as Ashok Kumar made it 2-1 in the 51st minute.

Now the late Jasdev Singh's voice on All India Radio was rising with excitement and emotion as India clung onto the lead and lifted the Cup under the able captaincy of Ajitpal Singh. Live television coverage? Keep dreaming! Doordarshan was still taking baby steps 16 years after its birth.

In fact it was exactly a month earlier in Calcutta that the first sporting event had been telecast live on the DD national hookup and shown in the major metro cities. That was the 33rd World Table Tennis championship which triggered a TT revolution in West Bengal. Before that the 1972-73 Bombay Test v England (MCC) had been shown within the city limits as were the five Tests against the visiting West Indies in 1974-75. But hockey? No chance!

In fact 1975 was a vintage year for two sports-crazy teens with the fag-end of that Test series which was not decided (3-2 in the tourists' favour) till the last day of the final Test, followed close on its heels by the World TT, then the World Cup hockey and after that in the summer, the inaugural (Prudential) World Cup cricket in England, all culminating with the start of the unofficial Test championship of the world, West Indies in Australia 1975-76. The icing on the cake from a personal point of view was my favourite Arthur Ashe outwitting defending champion, that upstart Jimmy Connors in the final of Wimbledon.

But we could not watch any of these live on our black-and-white TVs—which must come as a shock to the current generation with wall-to-wall 24x7 sports coverage on TV, online and on mobile apps.

India being in the final at Kuala Lumpur was not a total surprise. They had lost a heart-breaking final to hosts the Netherlands in 1973 though the last gold medal in the Olympics was back in 1964 in Tokyo. Cricket on the other hand was still licking its wounds after the ignominy of the 3-0 whitewash in England the previous year which almost wiped out memories of the unprecedented hat-trick of rubbers from 1971-73.

The Prudential World Cup started disastrously with a drubbing at the hands of England in the opening match at Lord's, a slight up-tick with a win over the unheralded and unknowns of East Africa (a team that would never be seen again) and then defeat to New Zealand seeing the end of a low-key campaign where expectations were low and curiosity high over the format (60 overs in England).

Hockey went downhill all the way from Kuala Lumpur. In the 1976 Montreal Olympics India failed to medal for the first time since making their debut in 1928, finishing a miserable seventh and in the 1978 World Cup in Buenos Aires the defending champions crashed to sixth place. Sadly, India has never even managed to reach the semifinals of the World Cup since 1975.

Limited-overs cricket had been introduced at the national domestic level for the first time in England in 1963 with the Gillette Cup, then of 65 overs per side. Once it was announced in 1973 that the first men's World Cup would be staged two years hence, the BCCI belatedly decided to introduce the first limited-overs national tournament, the Deodhar Trophy (60 overs; on a zonal basis) in the 1973-74 season. But the response was tepid at best. And if the Indians performed poorly in 1975, the next in England in 1979 was even worse as India suffered the ignominy of defeat at the hands of Sri Lanka who were still three years away from achieving Test status.

The first sports event abroad to be shown live was the Indian cricket team's tour to Pakistan in 1978 where India were beaten 2-0 in the three Tests. But the quantum leap in telecast technology came with New Delhi's staging of the Asian Games in 1982, the first multi-sports event to be held in India since the inaugural Asian Games in 1951.

By this time Sri Lanka (Rupavahini), Pakistan (PTV) and Bangladesh (BTV) were showing live international sports in colour. India on the other hand was at least a decade behind and India as the hosts of the Asiad had to arrange for live telecast facilities to the participating countries including such technologically advanced nations like Japan and South Korea. All 34 countries of the Asian Pacific Broadcasting Union had switched to colour and none were interested in relaying b/w pictures. Thus began the process to upgrade the moribund Doordarshan to colour and create a pan-India service.

As written in the 2008 book *Olympics: The India Story* by Boria Majumdar and Nalin Mehta: "The overhaul of Indian television and the creation of a televised national service was to unleash far-reaching changes in Indian society." That same year the FIFA World Cup staged in Spain was shown live in India for the first time (and we bought our first TV).

Back then the BCCI was lukewarm, to say the least about the whole concept of ODIs. Their reasoning was clear: why stage a match over just one day when Test matches over five (and sometimes six) was packing in the crowds? They had however from the 1980-81 season added another one-day tournament to the domestic calendar, rather reluctantly at that and only because it received generous sponsorship from the Wills tobacco group. The Wills Trophy was a 50-over-a-side event and at least gave the Indians a little more feel for the format.

However, it was not until 1981-82 that the Board deigned to stage the first ODIs in India. There were three against the English tourists, the first being staged at Ahmedabad on November 25, 1981. This was the same city where in February 2022 India became the first country to play 1,000 ODIs. Rather surprisingly, India won the series against England 2-1 but it slipped under the radar, hardly attracting much attention. The only other ODIs staged in India before the 1983 Prudential World Cup in England was when India made a clean sweep of the three against Sri Lanka in September 1982.

India surprised themselves as much as anyone by beating the mighty defending champions by 27 runs in the second ODI at Albion, Berbice in Guyana on the disastrous 1983 tour of West Indies. This gave the players a sense of self-belief before the England event. Still, the whole build-up to the third Prudential World Cup in June 1983 was as low-key as the previous two editions, at least for the Indians.

Mohinder Amaranth in his 2024 autobiography *Fearless: A Memoir* describes the scene: "The general atmosphere around the event indicated little interest from the BCCI. For them this World Cup was a mere formality and no more…I believe there was no farewell function [Amarnath was playing league cricket in England at the time] or even the token encouragement from the higher ups! The preparation for this event was the board's last priority, so they didn't bother holding any sort of preparatory camp. They felt it was an unnecessary expenditure. The press, cricket board and the general feelings among the cricket fraternity and followers was identical. They had little faith in the team due to their poor track record in the previous World Cups. No one expected any miracles from this team."

Truth to tell, even the team members themselves were reconciled to their fate. They had made bookings for a holiday in the United States where they would play exhibition matches to bring in some useful dollars. These dates were fixed for right after India's group stage matches. The thought of reaching the semifinals did not even enter their minds!

So imagine everyone's surprise, rather shock, when India made it all the way to the semifinals and then after stunning hosts England, pulled off the Miracle at Lord's in the final. This shocked not only the defending champions confident of a hat-trick of titles, but the Indians themselves and as well as the whole sporting world with one of history's greatest upsets on June 25, 1983.

All India Radio had not even sent a team of commentators for India's games. Back home we had to tune into BBC World Service on Short Wave to hear the commentary. Until the semifinal against England at Old Trafford, Manchester that is. Suddenly Doordarshan was spurred into action and hurriedly arranged with BBC TV to relay the telecast. That too in glorious colour even though the majority of TV owners were yet to upgrade their sets.

As for the final, even as the last West Indian wicket fell and all hell broke loose at Lord's, it was exactly midnight in India. DD flashed the anodyne headline 'India Wins' on our screens and we rushed out into the night to celebrate with family, friends and neighbors in scenes reminiscent of Jawaharlal Nehru's famous "at the stroke of the midnight hour" speech announcing the independence of India on August 15, 1947.

There are far too many **what ifs** to ponder over after all these years. But two of the pivotal moments centre round perhaps the only one in the team who in his heart of hearts felt India had a fighting chance before the World Cup, the inspirational captain Kapil Dev. He rescued India from a dire position and almost certain elimination in the return match against Zimbabwe at Tunbridge Wells, a ground that has since become something of a pilgrimage for Indians visiting England and has never again hosted an international match.

Then in the final, as Viv Richards disdainfully hoicked Madan Lal and commentator Richie Benaud simply said "shot" anticipating another boundary, Kapil at midwicket sprinted as if his life depended on it and plucked the ball out of thin air over his left shoulder, clutching it in his fingertips. Richards had already swatted six fours in his 33 and at 57 for two from 14 overs, Windies were cantering past India's measly 183. But their hopes sunk as seconds later Benaud deadpanned "not so good".

What if Kapil had not pulled off his second miracle of the World Cup? Windies would no doubt have made it three titles in a row and the World Cup would not have been prised out of England's grasp and brought to India and Pakistan four years later. But more on that anon.

This is where cricket stole a march over hockey—the unique aspects of the visual medium ensuring India's cricket glory overshadowed Indian hockey's which had only been heard over the 'wireless' eight years earlier. Kapil Dev thus went one better than Ajit Pal Singh for no fault of the legendary hockey captain.

To add to hockey's woes, the 7-1 thrashing at the hands of arch-rivals Pakistan in the final of the Asian Games the year before in front of the entire Indian political echelon was a humiliation it would take a generation to erase. The hockey gold was supposed to be the icing on the cake of two weeks of a glorious sporting spectacle brilliantly organized by the government. But this drubbing brought it crashing down to a bitter anti-climax with millions watching in their homes, some on their spanking new colour TV sets.

So even as Kapil's Devils (as the team became known) were feted and rewarded by the government and an ecstatic nation, the hapless goalkeeper Mir Ranjan Negi and his men slunk away in disgrace.

Nehru Saves Indian Cricket

Coming back to Nehru, it is fair to say his one act in 1950 saved Indian cricket at a time when it was facing stiff competition for popularity from football and hockey. This has been explained in two books by Mihir Bose, *A Maidan View: The Magic of Indian Cricket* and *The Nine Waves: The Extraordinary Story of Indian Cricket,* written three decades apart.

After India became a republic on January 26, 1950 there was pressure on Nehru, chiefly from Home Minister Sardar Vallabhai Patel to leave the Commonwealth group headed by the old colonial masters, Great Britain.

One of the main clauses of the-then Imperial Cricket Conference established in 1909 with England, Australia and South Africa as the founder-members was that membership of the ICC was predicated on nations being part of the Commonwealth. This was how Argentina and the United States missed out despite cricket being popular there back then.

Shrugging off the pressure from Patel and within his own Congress Party, Nehru decided to retain India's membership. He took a keen interest in cricket and like a shrewd politician saw it as a way to connect with the public. But whether his decision was at least partly motivated by a desire for India to retain ICC membership and Test status is not known. Leaving the Commonwealth would have meant automatic forfeiture of this status. And with no Test matches to sustain interest, cricket in India would surely have faded into oblivion. Certainly then a pivotal **'what if'** moment in the history of the nation and the sport.

(See also 'How Jawaharlal Nehru Saved Indian Cricket' by Gulu Ezekiel, *The Indian Express,* November 10, 2024. https:// indianexpress.com/article/opinion/columns/jawaharlal-nehru-indian-cricket-9654621/)

India the New Hosts

The domino effect of the Miracle at Lord's saw the World Cup removed from England after three consecutive editions and brought to the backyard of the upstarts of world cricket, India and Pakistan. It would not return to England till 1999.

The series of dramatic events was precipitated by a rebuff to India's 'pass culture' by the mandarins of the MCC, the custodians of Lord's. BCCI President and cabinet minister NKP Salve had been invited as a guest to the box of the MCC President for the final. But his request for four extra passes for relatives and an Indian politician and his wife was turned down by the MCC. This enraged Salve who perceived it as a snub and national insult and resolved there and then to challenge the authority of England and Australia who enjoyed veto power at the ICC.

The BCCI and the Board of Control for Cricket in Pakistan jointly bidding for and winning the rights to stage the 1987 Reliance World Cup would not have even been envisaged if not for India winning the title that June of 1983 and the perceived snub to Salve. At the July 1984 ICC meeting in London India and Pakistan won their joint bid against that of England's Test and County Cricket Board by 16 votes to 12... and the rest is cricket history.

Today if the ICC (International Cricket Council) is tongue-in-cheek referred to as the Indian Cricket Council it is in no small measure thanks to India (with Pakistan) becoming the first to break the monopoly of England and the World Cup. These events led to Jagmohan Dalmiya in 1997 being elected the first Asian head of the ICC, followed by N. Srinivasan, Shashank Manohar and the current incumbent, Jay Shah. India today is undoubtedly the financial powerhouse of world cricket. And all thanks to Kapil's Devils.

When Dalmiya assumed office in 1997, the ICC working out of a shabby office at Lord's, had little more than US $25,000 in its kitty;

by the time his term ended the canny businessman and administrator from Calcutta had transformed the world body into a multi-million dollar entity and its HQ is now a modern office block in Dubai. The anachronistic veto power long enjoyed by the Anglo-Australian bloc had been abolished in 1993, thus paving the way for new power blocs to emerge, led of course by the omnipotent BCCI.

But the real consequence of the new Asian influence happened thanks to the marketing nous of Dalmiya and Inderjit Singh Bindra. Together they broke the state's TV/Doordarshan monopoly after a bitter battle with the government in the law courts between 1992 and 1995. The TV rights bonanza from Mark Mascarenhas' WorldTel when the World Cup returned to India and Pakistan (with Sri Lanka as tri-hosts) in 1996 set the trend for billion dollar deals in the years to come.

In fact it was the 1996 Wills World Cup more than the 1987 Reliance World Cup which changed the face of ODIs. Now the Indian team was jetting all over the world playing bilateral and tri-nation tournaments in non-traditional centres like Sharjah, Toronto and Nairobi, sponsored by MNCs including Coca-Cola and Pepsi who had entered the Indian marketplace along with cable TV channels after the opening up of the economy in 1991.

The influx of big money coupled with the largely meaningless context of these matches brought in a sense of ennui and cynicism among the players and was a major reason behind the match fixing scandal that rocked the cricket world in 2000.

But with the launch of the mega-rich Indian Premier League in 2008, there is no going back on the fact that Indian cricket today powers the world cricket economy. So from the Indian perspective it is perhaps just as well that the request for those four passes for the 1983 Prudential World Cup final was turned down.

'Kapil drops Viv' was the headline to Gideon Haigh's 'what if' feature in *ESPN-Cricinfo's The Cricket Monthly* issue of January 2015 where Haigh speculated over the fate of the Lord's final as well as other seminal moments in world cricket history.

So **what if** Salve's request for those extra passes from the snooty MCC had been accepted? One can only speculate!

Over to 2007

Now fast forward 24 years to 2007, one of the most turbulent in Indian cricket history.

In short order: India beat West Indies and Sri Lanka in ODI series at home in January/February; India and Pakistan crash out in the first round of the World Cup in West Indies in March, leading to the sacking/resignation of coach Greg Chappell; the simultaneous announcement by Subhash Chandra of the Zee Telefilms network of his breakaway T-20 Indian Cricket League; India in Bangladesh in May win the Test series and in July-August win a Test series in England for the first time since 1986—Rahul Dravid then quits the captaincy; India win the inaugural World T20 in South Africa in September with captain Mahendra Singh Dhoni and the simultaneous announcement from BCCI of the launch of the Indian Premier League (IPL) in early 2008; India win the Test series at home against Pakistan in November-December under new captain Anil Kumble, the last time Pakistan play a Test in India; the start of the stormy tour of Australia in December 2007.

Phew! Just thinking back to those events makes the head spin. But it is the behind-the-scenes events that are just as dramatic.

India had not won the World Cup since that magical day at Lord's in 1983, the closest being in 2003 when they finished runners-up to Australia at Johannesburg. So the Indian public was hungry for another title. As had been the case every four years since 1983, the Indian team headed to West Indies in March 2007 with hopes high of another success.

India were placed in Group B with Sri Lanka and two apparent 'minnows', Bangladesh and debutants Bermuda. Pakistan was in Group D with West Indies, Ireland and Zimbabwe. The top two teams from the four groups would proceed to the 'Super 8' stage.

So confident were the organizers of both the Asian giants making it to the second stage, the ICC even drew up a pre-tournament schedule showing both India and Pakistan in the Super 8 stage. My objections to this was met with derision—of course both teams would advance!

India were slated to play their Super 8 matches in Barbados. The Barbados government sent representatives of their national tourism board with star attractions Joel Garner and Rev. Wes Hall to major cities around India to attract tourists to their island. In fact thousands of Indian and Pakistani fans based in the United States and Canada had already made airline and hotel bookings for those Super 8 matches.

Imagine the shock then when India were beaten by Bangladesh in their opening match at their favourite Port of Spain, Trinidad. And on the very same day Pakistan were stunned by Ireland in Kingston, Jamaica.

It was as if a massive earthquake had rocked the World Cup for now the unthinkable was possible—both India and Pakistan could and indeed were knocked out in the group stage with both losing two of their three matches. This threw the organizers into disarray and the economies of the Caribbean islands, so dependent on the tourism dollar, were severely impacted as Indian and Pakistani fans made frantic cancellations. Never again would the ICC risk such a calamity in the format.

Back home the TV channels who had invested heavily in the World Cup suddenly found themselves facing a calamitous situation with the massive ad revenue they were expecting plunging down a black hole. They had been whipping up nationalistic frenzy in the run up to the mega-event with cricket superstars from India and around the world paid hefty sums to be the in-studio experts. The whole tenor of the coverage suddenly changed from support to fury and shamefully the homes of some of the Indian players, including Dhoni's in Ranchi were stoned by hoodlums masquerading as fans.

The first victim of this calamity was coach Chappell who jumped before he was pushed. Then came the announcement that Zee's Chandra had signed up 50-plus players from India and around the world for his 20/20 rebel ICL to be launched in November 2007. The legendary Kapil Dev was recruited for a fabulous sum as consultant.

Ravi Shastri was roped in as interim coach for the tour of England, the Test series won 1-0 and the ODIs lost 4-3. Now came the drama of the inaugural World T20.

If India were lukewarm to the ODI World Cup for the first three editions (1975, 1979, 1983) they were even more so for the T20 version in South Africa in September 2007, then known as ICC World T20, now ICC T20 World Cup. The world event was to be launched just four years after the first T20 domestic competition in England in 2003 which proved an immediate and massive commercial success.

New Format

Australia's Malcolm Speed was CEO of the ICC from 2001 to 2008, the last vestige of the Anglo-Australian old guard in world cricket fighting a losing battle against the BCCI's rising power.

His animosity towards both Indian officialdom and Indian cricket (the feeling was mutual) was made clear in his 2011 autobiography *Sticky Wicket: Inside Ten Turbulent Years at the Top of World Cricket*.

Then BCCI Secretary Niranjan Shah's contention was Indian cricketers had not played Twenty20 and would thus be at a disadvantage.

The possibility of India losing co-hosting rights to the 2011 ODI World Cup was held out by the ICC if it refused to participate.

In the aftermath of the ICC meeting, *The Times of India* published a report by Chandresh Narayanan on February 18, 2006 headlined: 'India object to Twenty20 World Cup' in which he wrote: "At the ICC chief executives meeting in Dubai, India were the only dissenting voice against the new format being played for a World Cup. The BCCI has refused to play the inaugural event likely to be held next year."

BCCI vice-president Lalit Modi blustered: "If the ICC want to fine us, they can. We are ready to pay the fine, but we will not play the World Cup."

Wrote then-BCCI chief administrative officer Prof. Ratnakar Shetty in his 2022 *book On Board: Test. Trial. Triumph. My Years in BCCI*: "At this stage, the BCCI had made its view on Twenty20 (T20), the game's newest and shortest format, quiet clear. The Working Committee of the Board had opposed this format and opined that it would adversely affect the game in the long run as youngsters who played it would end up lacking in terms of technique, patience and application and consequently struggle in the traditional and multi-nuanced multi-day format." But they were out-voted at the 2006 ICC meeting and had to go along.

The BCCI now organized a domestic T20 tournament in the 2006-07 season, the last of the major member nations to do so to prepare the players for the inaugural World Cup. Initially called the Inter-State Twenty-20 Competition, it was later named the Syed Mushtaq Ali Trophy (SMAT).

Out of curiosity at this new format I went to the Feroze Shah Kotla ground in New Delhi to watch Delhi captained by Virender Sehwag take on (and lose to) Himachal Pradesh on April 3, 2007. Pleasantly surprised by the turnout—only in its hundreds, but far more than for a Ranji Trophy match—I turned to the late cricket official Sunil Dev and told him "if this format is expertly marketed, it could be a huge success." Dev just nodded in response. Little did I know it would become the behemoth it has now grown into with leagues scattered around the world and throughout the year and the mega success of the IPL making the BCCI one of the richest sporting associations in the world.

But coming back to the World T20, wonder of wonders, who would contest the final but those two reluctant participants, India and Pakistan?

The Indian team wore a young look. Right after the England tour the veterans, captain Dravid, Sachin Tendulkar and Sourav Ganguly expressed their inability to take part and the selection committee faced with many choices as captain—Gautam Gambhir, Sehwag and Yuvraj Singh among them—pulled off what would be a masterstroke by appointing Dhoni. It was a decision which would have far reaching ramifications beyond the WorldT20 and indeed change the whole complexion of Indian cricket.

India, captained by Sehwag, had played just one T20 International prior to this, beating South Africa by six wickets in Johannesburg in December 2006. It would be the lone T20 International match in the storied career of Tendulkar.

Dhoni's Daredevils

Now India was back at the same venue and edged Pakistan in the final to win the inaugural title. It was as if the pain of the ODI World Cup ignominy just six months earlier had been all but forgotten. The same Dhoni whose house was stoned was now the toast of the nation.

And while S. Sreesanth's catch to dismiss the final Pakistani batsman Misbah-ul-Haq was a sitter compared to Kapil's stunner to send back Richards 24 years earlier, both catches would result in cataclysmic changes to cricket's eco-structure. Earlier, it was Yuvraj's six 6s in an over by England's Stuart Broad that set the tournament alight.

Even as India was making its way to the final and interest for cricket's latest baby was reaching fever pitch, came the announcement by Lalit Modi that from early 2008 the BCCI would launch the Indian Premier League T20 tournament with eight franchises representing major cities around India.

While the ICL was the immediate catalyst, Modi's ambitious plans were in the works for some time and had been mooted at an ICC Commercial Forum meeting in 2006. Now Modi got the green signal from Sharad Pawar and cricket would never be the same again. As for the ICL launched in November 2007, just five months before the IPL, it folded up after only two seasons.

So **what if** India allied with Pakistan, had decided to forgo participation in the inaugural World T20 in South Africa in 2007? No doubt without the backing of Asian powers houses that tournament would then have been the first and last. And the fate of the IPL too would have been in doubt.

It was all said and done Dhoni's Daredevils who changed the face of world cricket in 2007 just as Kapil's Devils had done back in 1983.

CHAPTER TEN

The Changing Face of Cricket

Of Helmets and DRS

The late Bishan Bedi was one of cricket's most astute brains. The man with magic in his left arm had a favourite saying: "nothing has changed, the game has remained the same after all these years."

Bedi's contention was that cricket is still essentially a battle between bat and ball just as it had been way back in 1744 when the laws were first codified—nearly 300 years ago.

The legendary captain and spin bowler *par excellence* is correct in that regard. But in other aspects cricket has seen a sea-change over the last four decades.

Limited-overs matches? Corruption and fixing? The history of cricket has seen it all since it first started being played in the English countryside in the mid-1500s, before spreading across the rest of England and the world with the spread of colonialism over the centuries.

But two aspects of modern cricket would indeed be unrecognizable to anyone taking a time machine from even 50 years back to the present day—the use of helmets for batsmen and fielders/wicket-keepers and even occasionally, bowlers and umpires and the TV third umpire and DRS (Decision Review System) to assist in decisions.

While the first recognized Test match was staged at Melbourne between England and Australia in March 1877, it was not until 100 years later that professional cricket saw the introduction of the helmet for batsmen, something that had been common practice in baseball—cricket's American cousin. The very first cricketer to use this form of protection was England's opening batsman Dennis Amiss during the first season of Kerry Packer's World Series Cricket in late 1977. He was soon followed by England team-mates Alan Knott and Tony Greig and a whole host of others including South Africa's master opening batsman Barry Richards.

The immediate cause for this seismic shift in cricket was the injury suffered by Australia's dynamic young left-hander David Hookes as he missed an attempted hook and had his jaw smashed by a bouncer from West Indies' Andy Roberts, whose bouncer was considered the most lethal of all the fast bowling legends of that golden era of fast bowling. This happened during the second 'Supertest' between WSC Australians and WSC West Indians at the Sydney Showground in December 1977 and sent panic through the ranks as WSC laid heavy emphasis on fast bowling with no restriction on bouncers.

Hookes was one of WSC's marquee players in its inaugural season as it struggled to gain a foothold on the Australian cricket firmament. His loss for the season was a big blow to Packer's grand plans to upstage traditional Test cricket and the boss decided not to take chances of losing any more of his highly-paid stars. He placed a bulk order with a firm in England who were making modified motorcycle helmets and now with all the other innovations introduced by WSC—coloured clothing, the white ball, cricket under lights—came one more, though inadvertently.

It was not long before cricketers in the traditional game too took to the new implement. The pioneer in this regard was another Australian left-hander, Graham Yallop who wore the crash helmet in March 1978 on Australia's stormy tour of West Indies where Australia's third-string side, sans their WSC stars were up against the might of the home side, though only for the first two of the five Tests. Yallop's innovation came in the second Test at Bridgetown, Barbados where he scored 47 and 14. Hooted and taunted by the crowd, Yallop decided to discard the helmet in the tour match that followed against Guyana at Georgetown. The result: he had jaw broken by the fearsome Colin Croft in the first innings after scoring 118! This meant he missed the third Test at the same venue.

So many talented cricketers worldwide, Indians included, came and went for lack of proper protective gear and not only helmets. Even the leg-guards and gloves were of abysmal quality and could hardly stand up to the thunderbolts sent down by fast bowlers over the decades. The former England captain and opening batsman Mike Atherton wrote in his column in *The Times* (UK) that Test batsmen in the pre-helmet Test era (1877 to 1977) should have 10 added to their averages. In Atherton's words, back then the next ball bowled to a batsman could have been their last.

So **what if** such gear had been available before the late 1970s? How many of our otherwise talented batsmen brought up on placid tracks and a diet of spin bowling could have had fruitful careers if not for fear of serious injury? And at least one, Nari Contactor had his cruelly cut short by a fractured skull courtesy a Charlie Griffith bouncer. (Chapter 6).

Helmets first hit the headlines in India on the tour of Pakistan in 1978, the first series between the two countries in 17 years. This was the debut series for Kapil Dev and he made an immediate impact in the first Test at Faisalabad, bouncing opener Sadiq Mohammad who then called for the helmet. This was an unprecedented sight for Indian fans—the series was the first foreign sports event to be telecast live on *Doordarshan*. Imagine an Indian bowler inducing panic in the opposition ranks! Remember, we had not produced a genuine fast bowler since the days of Mohammad Nissar and L. Amar Singh in the 1930s.

India were touring Australia in 1977-78 with the traditional Test series running concurrently with Packer's young upstart. But despite having Jeff Thomson in the Aussie ranks, none of the batsmen called for the helmet. No doubt they were monitoring developments on Packer's Channel 9 with intense interest though.

It was not till their tour of England in 1979 though that helmets became popular with Indian batsmen with the late opener Chetan Chauhan being the first to don one. But even then there was some resistance as the early models were bulky and uncomfortable. Back then they were available either open-faced or with visors. The latter was soon discarded as the visors tended to get foggy, impairing vision. It was not till the mid-80s that the helmet with face grille became standard equipment around the world both for batting and close-in fielders.

On the 1980-81 tour of Australia with Dennis Lillee, Len Pascoe and Rodney Hogg in their ranks, Sandeep Patil suffered a serious head injury in the first Test at Sydney when struck by a Pascoe thunderbolt. Knocked unconscious and hospitalized he came storming back in the next Test at Adelaide—now armed with a helmet—with a blazing 174, his maiden Test hundred. Suitably protected, he smashed England's fast bowler Bob Willis for six fours in an over in the second Test at Old Trafford in 1982 on the way to his second century.

No one ever doubted Patil's courage and technique. Nor would anyone dare do so when it came to Mohinder Amarnath. But both were frank enough to admit in their books released in 2024 that the use of helmets made a huge difference to their confidence levels.

Helmets came in time for them and many others. But not for Contractor who almost lost his life in 1962. The late Aunshuman Gaekwad was struck on the left ear by Michael Holding, another life-threatening injury, in the notorious 'Bloodbath at Kingston' in 1976. He carried the after-effects of that injury throughout his life. Mind you, both Patil (on 65) and Gaekwad (81) were well set when struck.

So many careers came to a premature end before the late 1970s because Indian batsmen were unused to the pace and bounce of foreign pitches brought up as they were on Indian tracks which were placid with pace bowlers struggling to get lift and speed.

Just three examples out of so many would suffice: Brijesh Patel, Parthasarathy Sharma and Ashok Mankad. All three were master batsmen at home but struggled abroad. Patel did have one Test century to his credit but that he was susceptible to the quicks was an open secret even while he was a butcher of bowling at the domestic level.

Sharma had a good start to his Test career with 54 and 49 on debut against West Indies at New Delhi in 1974-75 but was found woefully lacking in technique outside India while Mankad had his best score of 97 in just his fifth Test against Australia at Delhi in 1969-70. He also had a sharp cricket brain and may have made a good Test captain. Sharma was so well thought of that he was appointed batting coach at the National Cricket Academy in Bangalore with Gautam Gambhir among others being his trainees.

As for Mankad, he is the owner of a remarkable first-class record—the highest average by a batsman in 18 or more innings at a single venue, 106.30 at the Wankhede Stadium in Bombay. At one time he was the owner of the record for most runs and centuries in the Ranji Trophy. But Sharma played his final Test in January 1977 and Mankad exactly a year later. **What if** helmets had been in vogue earlier, would they have made a qualitative difference to the Test careers of these domestic stalwarts and given the Indian batting precious assets?

Most remarkable is the story of Mohinder Amarnath who in the 1982-83 season had two of the most sensational Test series abroad in cricket history against top-quality fast bowling, of which there was plenty in that era, topping it off with a brilliant display in the third Prudential World Cup in England.

In Pakistan against Imran Khan and Sarfraz Nawaz and then in West Indies against perhaps the most potent fast bowling attack of all time—Holding, Roberts, Marshall and Joel Garner—Amarnath topped the aggregates and averages for India against Pakistan with 584 runs, average 73 and against West Indies with 598 runs, average 66.44. In fact in the latter he scored the most runs on either side, remarkable considering the wealth of batting in the West Indies line-up. That India lost both series (3-0 in six Tests in Pakistan, 2-0 in five in West Indies) speaks volumes as to how he was head-and-shoulders above the rest of the Indian batting. In those combined 11 Tests Amarnath recorded five centuries and seven half-centuries, an awesome achievement. Contrast this with just one century and four fifties combined in 10 Tests in Australia, Pakistan and England between 1977 to 1979. So what helped him make that quantum leap in form?

It was the series of injuries at the hands of the quicks between 1977 and 1979 that saw him don the helmet and change his stance, dramatically boosting both his confidence and run output. Sam Gannon in Australia in 1977-78, Imran Khan in Pakistan in 1978 and New Zealand's Richard Hadlee in a tour match against Nottinghamshire between the third and fourth Tests in England in 1979, all struck him on the head. Of these Hadlee's blow was the most serious, leading to a fractured skull. An impulsive hooker, his unprotected head became a target for the fast bowlers. He learned to play that shot from his father who advised his three sons never to take a backward step against the fast men. It got him plenty of runs but also exposed him to serious injury. In West Indies in 1976 when the use of helmets was yet to enter anyone's mind-space, Amarnath was fortunate to escape unscathed even as many Indian batsmen were battered, bruised and broken by the ferocious pace and aggression of Holding in particular.

Three months after the Hadlee injury, Amarnath was back in the Test arena in the sixth and final Test against Australia at Bombay. At the nets before the match he experimented with a locally made helmet but found it to be too heavy for comfort. Looking for something light, yet strong enough to protect his skull, he decided to wear his father Lala's *sola topi* (pith hat) which had been worn in Australia in 1947-48. Indeed, long before helmets made an appearance, many cricketers opted for this headgear as it also provided shade from the sun. But after facing just seven deliveries he shaped to hook a Rodney Hogg bouncer, slipped in the process and his bat hit the stumps to be out hit wicket for two. Now he had become the butt of jokes and taunts.

Fortunately for Amarnath, his Delhi teammate Madan Lal gave him a helmet which suited him. "I found that wearing a helmet increased my confidence", he wrote in his autobiography *Fearless*. But the ignominy of his Bombay dismissal and word on the cricket grapevine that he was susceptible to the short pitched ball saw him out of international cricket till the tour of Pakistan in 1982-83. Three precious years were lost to add to seven in the wilderness after his Test debut in 1969-70. But **what if** he had taken to the helmet earlier? Surely that skull injury would have been avoided and his confidence restored after the knocks from Gannon and Imran. And those three lost years would most likely have been avoided too.

A sad footnote: the tragic death of Australian prodigy Philip Hughes in a Sheffield Shield match in 2014, just three days before his 27th birthday after a hit on the head proves that while helmets can prevent injury, they are not fool-proof. Indeed, even with helmets there have been a fair share of head injuries over the last near-half century. The reason being the false sense of security it gives a batsman who pre-1977 would sway out of the way of bouncers. Now the helmet allows them to make flamboyant shots they could not have dreamed of in an earlier era. But the danger still remains.

The DRS Dilemma

'Accurate umpiring at last!' was the headline on the cover of the January 1993 edition of *Wisden Cricket Monthly* depicting Sachin Tendulkar being run out in the first Test against South Africa at Kingsmead, Durban in November 1992. The inset photo on the cover was captioned "'Third' umpire Cyril Mitchley by the red or green light switches."

The first Indian sports team to land in South Africa was indeed historical for both political and sporting reasons. South African fans were getting a taste of Test cricket for the first time since Australia toured in 1970, followed by a lengthy ban from international cricket (lifted in late 1991) because of the White-minority government's abhorrent apartheid policy.

When the team landed in South Africa manager Amrit Mathur was called to a meeting to discuss the playing conditions when South Africa's cricket supremo and former captain Dr. Aaron (Ali) Bacher dropped a bombshell. He suggested the use of a third (TV) umpire to decide on line calls, run outs and stumpings, something South Africa had successfully used in their domestic competitions during the years of exile. Fortunately Mathur and vice-captain Ravi Shastri, who accompanied him to the meeting, agreed and today it has become accepted practice at all international and many domestic matches as well.

Tendulkar has many firsts to his credit but perhaps being the first batsman to be given out via TV replays is not one he would particularly relish. It was fitting that the fielder involved was the young Jonty Rhodes who earlier that year in the World Cup match in Brisbane had caught the attention of the cricket world with his spectacular run out of Pakistan's Inzamam-ul-Haq. On-field umpire Karl Liebenberg signaled to third umpire Cyril Mitchley, both South Africans who flashed the green light which back then meant Tendulkar (11) was out.

For *Wisden Cricket Monthly* editor David Frith in particular it was the vindication of a ten-year campaign to introduce such technology to cricket. The campaign was triggered off by the reprieve given to Australian opener John Dyson before he had opened his account in the fifth and final Ashes Test in Sydney in 1982-83. Dyson batted for five hours before being out for 79; the Test was drawn and Australia won the series 2-1. The umpire was exposed by TV replays which showed Dyson well short of the crease when the stumps were broken and was the culmination of a series of blunders by the home umpires. In his editorial ('Help the umpire') in the March 1983 issue, Frith wrote: "The errors of judgment made by cricketers are the very essence of the sport, which depends for its charm as much upon uncertainty as anything else. But there should be no uncertainty about umpiring. It has to be reliable…Hang 'human fallibility' with its supposed beauty. When it ruins an Ashes-deciding Test match, having already spoiled the series, it has to go."

Frith was not the first to come up with the idea, though he was certainly the first to extensively campaign for its introduction. In 1974 the Australian-born cricketer and umpire Bill Alley was quoted as saying: "I think in years to come there will be a box with a green and red light—equipped with a playback camera—and when there is an lbw appeal the umpire will look up at the box and get approval or rejection of the appeal via the camera. Umpires will be there to count six balls in the over but it will be the electric eye which will make the decisions." This was reported by John Davies in *Sportsweek* ('Owzat—a magic eye will decide, forecasts Alley', May 26, 1974)

Frith suggested the two-way communication between the on-field and the assistant at the TV monitor (Third Umpire) should be discreet and confidential through an earpiece. That is far from the case today with the discussions heard around the ground and the world via TV, making it transparent and perhaps adding to the drama. "The gain will be that major matches will be conducted, in umpiring terms, on lines of almost unchallengeably fair scrutiny."

There was pushback however from the old school of umpiring including the venerable Dickie Bird and the Jamaican Steve Bucknor.

Unfortunately for the Indians Bucknor allowed his ego to get the better of him when he refused to "go upstairs" in the drawn second Test at Johannesburg when Rhodes was clearly run out. South Africa were in dire straits at 26 for four in the first innings. Rhodes had already been dropped on zero and now enjoyed another reprieve when on 28. Javagal Srinath from mid-off threw down the stumps and the Indians appealed for the wicket that would have made South Africa 61 for 5. Despite much pleading Bucknor remained unmoved. Match Referee Clive Lloyd said after the match: if the facility is there, it should be used." Bucknor apologized and the next day was quick to ask for a replay when Tendulkar almost ran out Meyrick Pringle.

But it was too late for the Indians. Rhodes scored 91, South Africa totaled 292, the Test was drawn and South Africa won the four-Test series 1-0. It could so easily have ended 1-1. This would be the start of a long-running saga of distrust and bitterness between Indian cricketers and Bucknor till it all came to a head in Sydney in January 2008. But before cricket moved into the electronic age, it first needed to move into neutral mode.

International cricket for more than a century remained one of the few sports worldwide that did not employ neutral officials. The question of home umpires favouring the home side had been the centre of more ill-feeling and controversy than any other aspect of cricket. Pakistan's captain Imran Khan took a stand unilaterally to bring in neutral umpires for the home series against West Indies in 1986-87 (Chapter Eight). The first such pair were the Indians VK Ramaswamy and Piloo Reporter. England's John Hampshire and John Holder stood in the four Tests when India visited Pakistan in 1989. These encounters had created much bad blood between the two nations who were trying to mend fences after a long period when cricket ties were suspended (as they are now too). The four Tests were drawn and the neutral umpires played a very positive role in this.

But just six months before the Sydney Test almost led to a split in the cricket world, India's arch-nemesis came to India's aid. This was in the first Test at Lord's in July 2007. With the last wicket pair of Mahendra Singh Dhoni and S. Sreesanth grimly hanging on for a draw, left-arm spinner Monty Panesar and the entire England team went up in appeal for what looked on the replays to be a plumb lbw against Sreesanth. But Bucknor turned down the appeal and the match was drawn. India won the second at Trent Bridge and the third and final was drawn for captain Rahul Dravid to claim the series 1-0, a Test rubber win in England for only the third time following 1971 and 1986. India have yet to win a series in England since then at the time of writing and they have Bucknor to thank for that in 2007.

It was in 2007-08 when India toured Australia for the Border—Gavaskar Trophy that Bucknor found himself at the centre of an international storm. After Australia won the opening Test at Melbourne, the teams headed to Sydney in the New Year. A number of umpiring decisions went against the Indians with umpire Mark Benson of England and Bucknor under a harsh spotlight.

The most blatant of these came with Australia struggling to repair the first innings early damage of 134 for 6, Andrew Symonds at 30 edged Ishant Sharma to be caught behind by Dhoni. Seemingly everyone at the ground save for Bucknor heard the nick and to the dismay of the Indians the umpire was unmoved. Symonds top scored with 162 and Australia recovered to 463. India took a lead of 69 runs but set 333 to win, they collapsed to 210 to go two-down in the series. Both Dravid and Sourav Ganguly were given out to highly dubious catches in the second innings. But it was during the partnership of 129 runs between Sachin Tendulkar and Harbhajan Singh for the eighth wicket that a row ignited with Symonds who was of part Afro-Caribbean ancestry, alleging Harbhajan used a racial slur against him.

Match Referee Mike Procter slapped a three-Test ban on the off spinner after a lengthy hearing stretching into the middle of the night at the end of the Test. The BCCI appealed the ban and this is where things got murky. Meanwhile, the Indian team rallied behind their team-mate and there were threats the tour would be boycotted if Harbhajan's ban was not rescinded. The matter had even reached top diplomatic levels.

The ICC appointed New Zealand High Court judge Justice John Hansen to take evidence from players of both sides who were in proximity to the confrontation. Crucially the stump mic had not picked up what had been spoken by Harbhajan and he was let off with a fine for lack of concrete evidence.

However, the ICC made a crucial blunder at the hearing which came to India's aid—they had failed to provide Justice Hansen with the full extent of Harbhajan's past disciplinary record.

ICC CEO Malcolm Speed was in the thick of things. In his 2013 autobiography *Sticky Wicket* he writes of his reaction to the blunder: "I was very unhappy. I kicked my desk when I heard about it, hurting my foot..."

The first of Harbhajan's penalties had been imposed in the very first ODI tournament he took part in as a teenager in Sharjah in April 1998, his fourth ODI in a career stretching to 236 matches and less than a month after he had made his Test debut. It happened in the Coca Cola Cup tri-series also involving New Zealand and Australia. After having Ricky Ponting stumped, he gestured the batsman towards the pavilion for which he was fined 50 per cent of his match fee. This was in the famous 'Desert Storm' match in which Tendulkar's century took India to the final also against Australia which India won and in which he scored another century. Harbhajan did not play in the final. In 2005 he was fined 25 per cent of his match fee for a similar offence.

In his 2013 autobiography *At Close of Play* Ponting wrote of the incident. "My mood wasn't helped [at being stumped] when I looked up and found him right in my face, abusing me, telling me where to go."

This and two other infractions were not brought to Justice Hansen's attention by the ICC senior in-house lawyer Urvasi Naidoo, according to Speed. The crucial one that fell in this category happened during the infamous 2001 Port Elizabeth Test in South Africa when Match Referee Mike Denness sanctioned Harbhajan as well as five other Indian players for various offences. The 2001 offence was listed, but with four players grouped together, Naidoo missed the reference to Harbhajan, according to Speed. The offence was the most serious of the four—he was convicted of showing dissent at the umpire's decision and trying to intimidate the umpire for which he was fined 75 per cent of his match fee and given a suspended sentence of a one-Test ban.

So **what if** the ICC had not slipped up? Justice Hansen was angry. He said the 1998 and 2005 offences would not have made any difference to the penalty, but added: "However, if I had been made aware of the serious transgression in November 2001, I would have required more extensive submissions as to the offense in mitigation which could have led to a different penalty."

In plain language, Harbhajan would have faced a ban. Would that have led to the team boycotting the rest of the tour? The Test series was over but the Commonwealth Bank ODI tri-series remained. The financial consequences would have been disastrous for Cricket Australia, particularly with the inaugural Indian Premier League and Champions Trophy lined up in 2008 for which CA had a large financial stake. Many of the Australian cricketers also looked to make a small personal fortune in the IPL. A major split in the cricket world had thus been averted by an error. This was the second time after 2001 when the BCCI and the ICC were locked in an eyeball-to-eyeball confrontation. India were the financial powerhouse of cricket back then and even more today and neither the South African nor the Australian boards could stand up to their might.

The immediate fallout of the umpiring blunders was the introduction of the DRS, initially called UDRS (Umpires Decision Review System) and first used in the India in Sri Lanka Test series in July-August 2008, won 2-1 by the hosts. So something good came out of that sorry episode after all. But **what if** both the umpires had not made repeated howlers at Sydney, badly affecting India's chances to win their first series in Australia? Would DRS have been indefinitely delayed or even shelved altogether?

The idea was to eliminate umpiring howlers. However, it did not work out well for the Indians—of the 12 decisions over-ruled only one went in favour of the touring team. In all there were 48 reviews in the three Tests, 39 for lbw, including seven of the 12 successful ones. There were certainly initial flaws to be ironed out and India captain Anil Kumble said as much. "There are still teething problems in the technology…it is not 100%, that's for sure," he noted. For the lbw calls, the umpires were assisted by the ball tracking technology known as Hawk-Eye.

To opener Virender Sehwag fell the dubious distinction in the first Test in Colombo (SSC) of being the first batsman to be given ruled out via DRS, just as Tendulkar had been the first to be out via the Third (TV) Umpire in South Africa in 1992. Muthiah Muralitharan's appeal for lbw was turned down by the on-field umpire but on referral the decision was over-turned and Sehwag was on his way for 13 in the second innings. But the Indians were not happy with the process and thus was planted the first seeds of doubt. Kumble at Colombo became the first captain in Test history to call for the DRS, but that appeal proved unsuccessful while his counterpart Mahela Jayawardene was much more successful. In the first Test in which India were routed by an innings and 239 runs within four days it was spinners Murali and new cap Ajantha Mendis who did all the damage and in this they were assisted by three DRS calls going their way. DRS was officially launched by the ICC during the first Test between Pakistan and New Zealand in Dunedin in November 2009.

So for the first time in cricket history the batsmen would not get the traditional benefit of the doubt from umpires like Dickie Bird who were notorious for turning down lbw appeals, much to the consternation of bowlers.

The fallout of this series was the BCCI with the backing of their players refused to allow the use of DRS in bilateral series for the next eight years, the only country to take this stand. They did however win both the 2011 World Cup and 2013 Champions Trophy, both under the aegis of ICC, with DRS in place. The main issue was doubts regarding the accuracy of the ball-tracking Hawkeye tech when it came to the lbw. However they finally agreed to use it on a trial basis in the 2016-17 home series against England and since then it has become standard practice. It was new captain Virat Kohli who was in favour of the technology and this swayed the Board's views. His predecessors, Kumble and Dhoni were both DRS skeptics.

The July 2008 Colombo Test was Test number 1,882 since the first in 1877. **What if** the technology had been around since the start? Here we are entering the realms of science fiction and is beyond the scope of this book since there would be countless innings and Tests which would have been affected. *The Cricketer* gave it a go in their May 2016 issue. 'What if DRS had been around forever?' they asked eight English writers who predictably enough chose eight English scenarios, only one of which involved an India Test. In the same issue master fast bowler James Anderson wrote how Hawk-Eye technology helped him become England's leading wicket-taker thanks to the data and video it provided him with while the then-editor and former Middlesex pace bowler Simon Hughes explored how cricket had become the leading sport in the world in the use of technology, both in its TV coverage and assistance to players and umpires. All this was part of the magazine's 'Technology Special' which ran to 15 pages.

NOTABLE OFF SPINNERS : IMPACT OF LBW DECISIONS PRE & POST DRS								
POST WAR	Period	Tests	Wkts	LBW	% LBW	Avg	Econ	SR
JC Laker	1948-1959	46	193	32	16.58	21.24	2.04	62.3
LR Gibbs	1958-1976	79	309	21	6.80	29.09	1.98	87.7
EAS Prasanna	1962-1978	49	189	25	13.23	30.38	2.4	75.9
S. Venkataraghavan	1965-1983	57	156	24	15.38	36.11	2.27	95.3
S.N.Yadav	1979-1987	35	102	8	7.84	35.09	2.56	81.9
PRE 2009 DRS								
M.Muralidharan	1992-2010	133	800	150	18.75	22.72	2.47	55
Saqlain M	1995-2004	49	208	35	16.83	29.83	2.64	67.6
Harbhajan Singh	1998-2015	103	417	68	16.31	32.46	2.84	68.5
INTRO 2009 DRS								
GP Swann	2008-2013	60	255	70	27.45	29.96	2.98	60.1
NM Lyon	2011-2025	134	539	84	15.58	30.39	2.93	62.1
S.Ajmal	2009-2014	35	178	59	33.15	28.1	2.58	65.1
MM Ali	2014-2023	68	204	39	19.12	37.31	3.62	61.8
R Ashwin *	2011-2024	106	537	117	21.79	24	2.83	50.7
POST IND DRS 2016								
R Ashwin	2016-2024	67	317	62	19.56	23.8	2.76	51.5
** DRS in India fm 2016*								

Chart by Krishna Jaga

Perhaps the most hard-done-by are the off spinners of yore **(See chart above).** The likes of Lance Gibbs, S. Venkataraghavan and EAS Prasanna can only look on wistfully as Hawk-Eye allied with DRS helps the post-2008 generation of their ilk with one lbw after another, fattening their career records. I rolled my eyes in exasperation when someone tweeted Graeme Swann was a better off spinner than Jim Laker because of his superior Strike-Rate. In fact the difference is marginal. But when it comes to lbw dismissals, Swann's percentage is nearly double that of Laker.

Even with left-arm spinners of the pre-DRS/Hawk-Eye era, their lbw percentage is remarkably low— Derek Underwood (297 wickets/86 Tests; 24 lbw dismissals=8.8%); Bishan Bedi (67/266; 16=6.01%); Hedley Verity (40/144; 18=12.5% Sri Lanka's Rangana Herath is the record holder for most wickets by a left-arm spinner, 433 in 93 Tests. His lbw record is staggering: 108 lbw=24.94% . For Ravindra Jadeja: 80 Tests; 323 wickets; 60 lbw=18.57%; Daniel Vettori: 113 Tests; 362 wickets; 76 lbw=20.99%

So just like helmets divide batsmen between the pre (1877 to 1977) and post-generation (1978 till today), so too DRS/Hawk-Eye for the bowler, particularly spinner, traditionally looked down upon as the poor cousin of cricket, who now has a level playing field without the benefit automatically going the pampered batsmen's way. No more notorious padding away of spin bowling like Peter May and Colin Cowdrey who put the West Indies spin bogey to rest during their mammoth stand at Edgbaston in 1957. Or West Indies' wicket-keeper/batsman Jimmy 'Padams' Adams fattening his batting stats by using his pads more than his bat. DRS and Hawk-Eye has sorted that lot out once and for all!

What if indeed!

Note: I am indebted to Bengaluru-based cricket analyst Krishna Jaga for working out the data for the lbw chart.

Acknowledgements

Sachin Bajaj; Deborah Best (National Archives of Trinidad and Tobago); Raj Bhat; Trinanjan Chakraborty; Martin Chandler; Dharmenderr Chaudhury; Lucia Chudikova; Peter Cullivan; Pritam Ghosh; Ramachandra Guha; Carolyn Gupta; Joseph Hoover; Krishna Jaga; Neeran Karnik; Saumil Kapadia; Nasser Khan; Prasanth Kiran; Marcus Lee; Steven Lynch; Nawaz Mody (KR Cama Oriental Institute Mumbai); Ian Subash Mohan; Clayton Murzello; Prof. Nigel Pyne; Rajdeep Sardesai; Prof. Nandini Sardesai; Gaurav Sethi; Rameshwar Singh; Mainak Sinha; B. Sreeram; Vincent Sunder; Tushar Trivedi.

Bibliography

Ricky Ponting: *At the Close of Play: My Autobiography* (Harper Collins, 2013)

Amrit Mathur: *Pitchside: My Life in Indian Cricket* (Westland Books, Chennai, 2023)

Sandeep Patil with Clayton Murzello: *Beyond Boundaries* (A Sachin Bajaj Publication/Global Cricket School, Mumbai, 2024)

Mohinder Amarnath with Rajendar Amarnath: *Fearless: A Memoir (*Harper Sport, New Delhi, 2024)

EAS Prasanna: *One More Over: An Autobiography* (Rupa, 1977)

Frank Tyson: *The Hapless Hookers* (Gary Sparke & Associates, Victoria, Australia, 1976)

S. Giridhar and VJ Raghunath: *Mid-Wicket Tales: From Trumper to Tendulkar* (Sage Publications, New Delhi, 2014)

Kishore Bhimani: *West Indies'76:India's Caribbean Adventure*

(Nachiketa Publications, Calcutta,1976)

Kishore Bhimani: *Director's Special Book of Cricketing Controversies* (Allied Publishers, Mumbai, 1992)

Viv Richards with Trevor McDonald: *The Authorised Biography*

(Belham Books, London,1984)

Viv Richards with David Foot: *Viv Richards* (World's Work Ltd, Surrey, 1979)

Vivian Richards with Bob Thomas: *Sir Vivian: The Definitive Autobiography* (Michael Joseph, London, 2000)

Partab Ramchand: *The Gentle Executioners: Story of Indian Spinners* (Konark Publishers, New Delhi, 2004)

Partab Ramchand: *Indian Cricket: The Captains: Nayudu to Tendulkar* (Marine Sports, Mumbai, 2004)

Sunil Gavaskar: Idols (Rupa & Co, 1985)

MV Gothoskar with Dr. AG Bhagwat: *The Burning Finger: An Indian Umpire Looks Back* (Marine Sports, Bombay, 1992)

Gideon Haigh: *The Cricket War: The Story of Kerry Packer's World Series Cricket* (Bloomsbury, London, 1993)

Sunder Rajan: *India vs West Indies 1974–75* (Jaico Books, Bombay, 1976)

Gallery

Chapter One

JM Framjee Patel. Courtesy Dr. Nawaz B. Mody, editor, Enduring Legacy (Vol. IV, page 1,068)

ME Pavri. From Parsi Cricket by ME Pavri. Courtesy: The Trustees, The K R Cama Oriental Institute, Mumbai

Ranji

GF Vernon, captain of the first team from England to tour India.

Chapter Two

Cover of the official BCCI souvenir for the 1932 tour of England.

Preliminary List of Players.

Any change will be duly announced.   Match Cards will be issued as soon as possible after the Captains have tossed.

2d. Lord's MCC Ground

ENGLAND v. ALL INDIA.

SATURDAY, JUNE 25, 1932.   (Three-day Match.)

ENGLAND.		First Innings.	Second Innings.
1 Sutcliffe	Yorkshire	B. NISSAR 3	
2 Holmes	Yorkshire	B. NISSAR 6	
3 Woolley	Kent	RUN OUT 9	
4 Hammond	Gloucestershire	B. AMAR SINGH 35	
5 D. R. Jardine	Surrey	CT. NAULE B NAYUDU 79	
6 Paynter	Lancashire	B. NAYUDU 14	
7 Ames	Kent	B NISSAR 65	
8 R. W. V. Robins	Middlesex	CT LALL SINGH B NISSAR 21	
9 F. R. Brown	Surrey	CT. AMAR SINGH B NISSAR 1	
10 Voce	Nottinghamshire	NOT OUT 4	
11 Bowes	Yorkshire	CT NISSAR B AMAR SINGH 4	

B , l-b , w , n-b ,   B , l-b , w , n-b ,

Total ...... 259 Total ......

FALL OF THE WICKETS.

1. 8 2. 11 3. 19 4. 101 5. 149 6. 166 7. 230 8. 231 9. 252 10.

ANALYSIS OF BOWLING.

Name.		1st Innings.						2nd Innings.					
		O.	M.	R.	W.	Wd.	N-b.	O.	M.	R.	W.	Wd.	N-b.
NISSAR													
AMAR SINGH													
KHAN													
PHIA													
NAYUDU													
N JEOOMAL													
N NAZIR ALI													

ALL INDIA.		First Innings.	Second Innings.
1 J. G. Navle	Gwalior		
2 Naoomal Jeoomal	Karachi		
3 S. Wazir Ali	Bhopal		
4 Capt. C. K. Nayudu	Indore		
5 S. H. M. Colah	Bombay		
6 S. Nazir Ali	Patiala		
7 P. E. Palia	Mysore		
8 Lall Singh	Kuala Lumpur		
9 Jahangir Khan	Jullundur		
10 L. Amar Singh	Jamnagar		
11 M. Nissar	Punjab		

B , l-b , w , n-b ,   B , l-b , w , n-b ,

Total ...... Total ......

FALL OF THE WICKETS.

1. 2. 3. 4. 5. 6. 7. 8. 9. 10.

1. 2. 3. 4. 5. 6. 7. 8. 9. 10.

ANALYSIS OF BOWLING.

Name.	1st Innings.	2nd Innings.

Umpires—Chester and Hardstaff.   Scorers—Maving and Martin.

The figures on the Scoring Board indicate the batsmen who are in.

Play begins 1st day at 11.30, 2nd and 3rd days at 11.

Luncheon at 1.30.   †Captain.   *Wicket-keeper.

Stumps drawn at 6.30 each day.

TEA INTERVAL.—There will probably be a Tea Interval at 4.30–4.45 but it will depend on the state of the game.

Original scorecard for India's maiden Test at Lord's.

India's first Test captain CK Nayudu.

The schoolboy Nawab of Pataudi, Iftikhar Ali Khan taking batting tips from Frank Woolley in London in December 1926.

Vijay Merchant.

Official BCCI souvenir for the 1946 tour of England.

Chapter Three

The author with Lala Amarnath, New Delhi, 1997.

Sir Donald Bradman

Fazal Mahmood

Dattu Phadkar

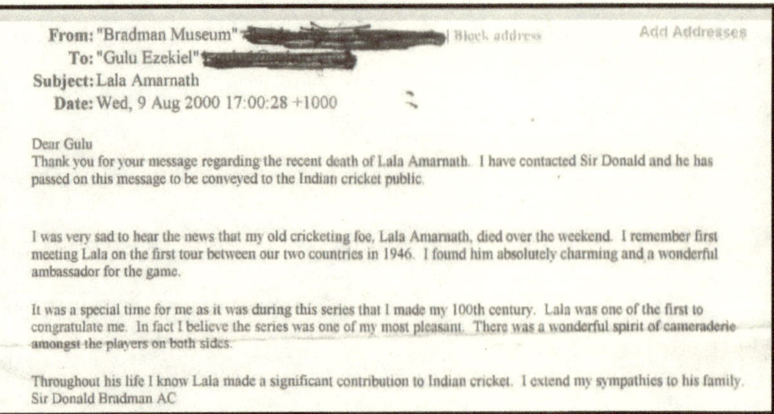

From: "Bradman Museum" ~~~~~~~~~~~~~~~~ | Block address   Add Addresses
To: "Gulu Ezekiel" ~~~~~~~~~~~~~~~~
Subject: Lala Amarnath
Date: Wed, 9 Aug 2000 17:00:28 +1000

Dear Gulu

Thank you for your message regarding the recent death of Lala Amarnath. I have contacted Sir Donald and he has passed on this message to be conveyed to the Indian cricket public.

I was very sad to hear the news that my old cricketing foe, Lala Amarnath, died over the weekend. I remember first meeting Lala on the first tour between our two countries in 1946. I found him absolutely charming and a wonderful ambassador for the game.

It was a special time for me as it was during this series that I made my 100th century. Lala was one of the first to congratulate me. In fact I believe the series was one of my most pleasant. There was a wonderful spirit of cameraderie amongst the players on both sides.

Throughout his life I know Lala made a significant contribution to Indian cricket. I extend my sympathies to his family.
Sir Donald Bradman AC

Condolence message from Sir Donald Bradman on the passing of Lala Amarnath. Message conveyed to the author via the Bradman Museum, Bowral, New South Wales.

Chapter Four

Jasu Patel

Salim Durani at the Sawai Man Singh, stadium in Jaipur in 2006.. Photo by Rameshwar Singh

Chapter Five

The spot at Hove near the statue of Queen Victoria where the accident involving Robin Waters and Tiger Pataudi occurred in July 1961. Photo by Lucia Chudikova

Tiger Pataudi at his wedding with Sharmila Tagore in 1968, here seen greeting late actor Sanjeev Kumar.

Chapter Six

Master leg spinner Subhash Gupte.

Nari Contractor

The Indian team to West Indies 1971. Skipper Ajit Wadekar is seated in the centre. Sunil Gavaskar is standing second from right. Photo by Gopal Bhat; Courtesy Raj Bhat

K. Jayantilal is brilliantly caught by Garry Sobers in the Indian opener's first and only innings in Test cricket, first Test at Kingston, Jamaica, 1971.

Dilip Sardesai, Indian cricket's "Renaissance Man' and one of the heroes of India's maiden victory in West Indies in 1971. Courtesy Prof. Nandini Sardesai

Sunil Gavaskar with Carolyn Gupte at the launch of her book on her parents Subhash and Carol Gupte at Queen's Park Oval, Port of Spain in 2019. Photo by Ian Subash Mohan

Chapter Seven

Lawrence Rowe falls on his stumps and is out hit wicket to Karsan Ghavri in the opening match of the 1974–75 tour of India v West Zone at Poona. Photo by Hosey Mistry

The catch that wasn't. Bowler S. Venkataraghavan, wicket-keeper Farokh Engineer and first slip GR Vishwanath appeal for a caught behind as batsman Viv Richards and non-striker Alvin Kallicharran await the decision. Umpire MV Gothoskar was unmoved.

Dr. Narottam Puri interviews West Indies captain Clive Lloyd after the December 1974 New Delhi Test. Looking on is the Indian captain. Photo courtesy Dr. Narottam Puri

Vivian Richards

Lawrence Rowe gets a pat from Dennis Lillee as he departs after his brilliant 175 for WSC West Indies v WSC Australia in the 'Supertest' at VFL Park, Melbourne in January 1979.

Chapter Eight

Queen's Park Oval, Port of Spain, Trinidad in 2013. Photo by Ian Subash Mohan.

Author (extreme right) with late Indian captain Bishan Singh Bedi, New Delhi, 1999.

Fast bowler Ian Bishop featured on a stamp issued by Trinidad & Tobago in 2003.

Dilip Vengsarkar (second from left) with (from right) Ravi Shastri, Sanjay Manjrekar, Balwinder Singh Sandhu, Pravin Amre and Prof. Ratnakar Shetty at the launch of Sandeep Patil's autobiography Beyond Boundaries with Clayton Murzello at CCI, Mumbai in November 2024.
Photo by Fotocorp

K. Srikkanth (right) with veteran cricket journalist R. Mohan at a function in Chennai.
Photo courtesy R. Mohan

Chapter Nine

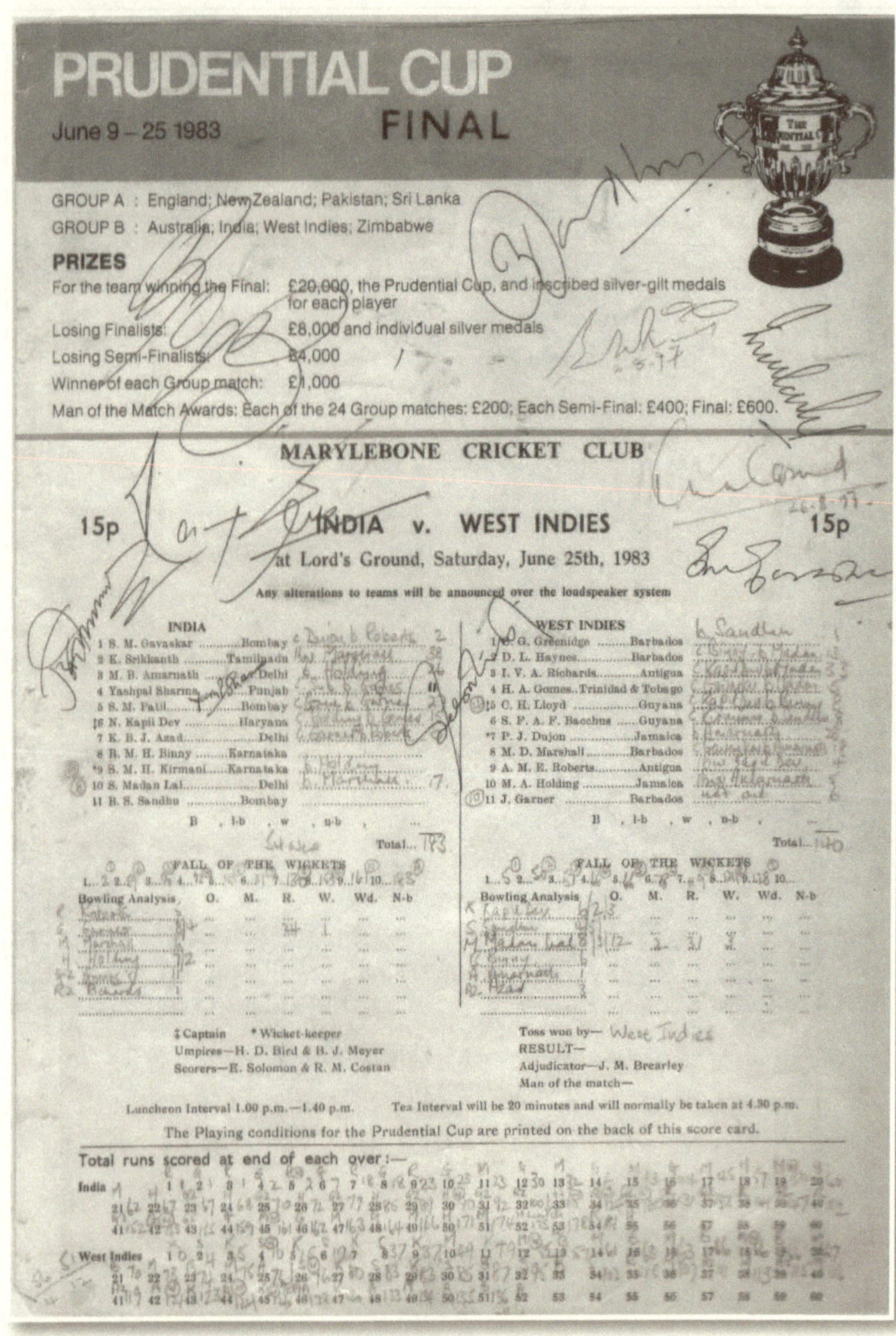

Original scorecard of the 1983 Prudential World Cup final at Lord's signed by the winning team

Members of the 1983 Prudential World Cup team at Ahmedabad airport in 2023. From left: Balwinder Singh Sandhu, Sunil Valson, captain Kapil Dev, K. Srikkanth, Roger Binny, Dilip Vengsarkar, Madan Lal and Sandeep Patil. Photo courtesy Sunil Valson

Chapter Ten

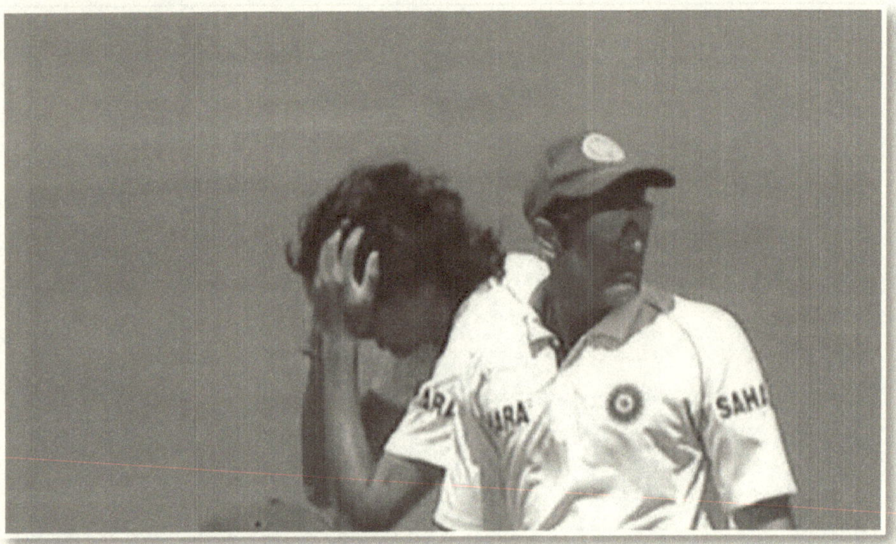

Bowler Ishant Sharma in despair and captain Anil Kumble in disbelief as umpire Steve Bucknor turns down the appeal for caught behind the wicket against Australia's Andrew Symonds; 2nd Test at Sydney, January 2008. Screen grab courtesy Mainak Sinha

Caricature by Gaurav Sethi on Steve Bucknor's retirement, first appeared on his website boredcricket.com in June, 2010